Etched
in
Purple

Related Titles from Potomac Books

Brassey's D-Day Encyclopedia:
The Normandy Invasion A–Z
by Barrett Tillman

The Forgotten Soldier
by Guy Sajer

Nuts!: The Battle of the Bulge
by Donald Goldstein, Katherine V. Dillon,
and J. Michael Wenger

Patton at Bay: The Lorraine Campaign, 1944
by John Nelson Rickard

Patton's Photographs: War as He Saw It
by Kevin M. Hymel

Strike and Hold: A Memoir of the 82ⁿᵈ Airborne in
World War II by T. Moffatt Burriss

Taught to Kill: An American Boy's War
from the Ardennes to Berlin
by John B. Babcock

Worshipping the Myths of World War II:
Reflections on America's Dedication to War
by Edward W. Wood, Jr.

Etched in Purple

One Man's War in Europe

Frank J. Irgang

Potomac Books
An imprint of the University of Nebraska Press

Library of Congress Cataloging-in-Publication Data
Irgang, Frank J.
    Etched in purple : one man's war in Europe / Frank J. Irgang. —
    1st ed.
        p. cm.
    Originally published: Caldwell, Idaho : Caxton Printers, 1949.
    ISBN 978-1-59797-204-8 (alk. paper)
    1. Irgang, Frank J. 2. World War, 1939–1945—Campaigns—
Western Front. 3. World War, 1939–1945—Personal narratives,
American. 4. Soldiers—United States—Biography. I. Title.
    D756.I74 2008
    940.54'1273092—dc22
    [B]
                                                      2007052987

Printed in the United States of America on acid-free paper that meets the American National Standards Institute Z39-48 Standard.

First Edition

Dedicated to the thousands of
young men and women
cheated of a
tomorrow

Etched
in
Purple

I.

THE crimson colors of a dipping sun shimmered in the well-sheltered English Channel harbor. The glinting waves were much smaller than the large, rolling surges that had rose and sunk beneath our ship during the long voyage to England.

After I had clambered into our landing craft I looked over the shoulders of my tense soldier comrades and saw ships of all shapes and sizes scattered over the bright waters as far as the eyes could see.

As the sun lowered behind the high mainland hills lights began to blink and flicker in the little English town through which we had just passed. Someone had told me it was Weymouth. The troops that had been billeted here predicted knowingly that this movement was just another invasion maneuver for they had gone through them several times in the past weeks and months. Once a German patrol boat had sunk two of their craft.

I was aid man for Company D, an infantry heavy weapons group. My job was to administer first aid and look after the general medical welfare of forty-two men. Tonight they seemed an especially large and burly lot, what with being loaded down with machine guns, mortars, and ammunition. I had seen thousands of husky troops in training in the United States, but none of them had appeared as tough as these. It's odd what a load of equipment and rations, properly distributed, can do to make an average soldier look like a bristling beast of war.

We had each received a carton of cigarettes. Since I did not smoke I passed mine around to the men of my platoon. Most of them grabbed them up eagerly. I found that this friendly gesture brought me closer to the fellows beside whom I was to spend the next days, weeks, or perhaps months. They began at once to call me "Doc," and I felt I now belonged as I crouched down on the deck of the boat and chatted with them. We all agreed in short time that the infantry was a sad spot with a war going on.

I was awakened by the gentle roll and the engine vibration of the moving vessel. Since most of the fellows were standing I lifted myself up and looked around. We seemed to be well out to sea. The sky was a dull gray. The dark water was chopped by a sharp and chilling breeze.

In the midafternoon scattered showers of gusty rain added shivers to the shakes we already had from the thought of what might lay ahead. Our officer in charge told us that we were about to invade France. Even now we could hear the roar of distant big guns. I was already seasick, but this news brought a sharp cramp to my stomach.

We were getting close to shore. The shells of the big guns of the many naval vessels behind us whispered a fearsome language as they zoomed overhead. We could hear explosions as they struck the mainland ahead. Soon

2

we heard the muffled booming of American field pieces already on shore.

Suddenly, the whistling scream of an incoming enemy shell sent all of us diving for the deck. I remembered then with a painful start that the enemy fights back. I was more frightened than I had ever been before. I knew now that I was afraid to die. I had never realized this so sharply before.

Great geysers of water spouted up all around us as the shells fell thickly. I looked for a shelter on the deck. In training I had been oriented on finding and taking cover on the ground, but not on a pitching ship. I wanted to jump off the craft, but the water was too deep. Besides, I had to wait for the order.

An infantryman on my right side was blown to bits in the midst of his comrades. An enemy bullet had set off a hand grenade which hung from his pack harness. I could see through the smoke that it had injured several others.

The blue haze had hardly cleared when another shell came screaming in. I dropped to the deck of our craft and waited for the shattering explosion. When at last it came, in a terrific burst, scraps of debris fell upon us. After I was sure it was over I slowly got up to my feet. The landing craft on our right had all but disappeared. Bloody fragments of it lay in our ship. My heart thundered. I clutched the side of the ship until my fingernails were blue.

Our ship came to a jarring stop as it thumped against a concrete obstacle. The order was given to get to the beach—every man for himself. I jumped over the side into water much deeper than I had expected. I sank up to my chest and began to struggle toward shore in the slimy beach water. My feet continually became entangled in the weeds and wire on the rocky bottom. Enemy shells were splashing among the struggling soldiers plunging toward the beach, but some of the men were out so far that it was impossible for them to make it. They yowled for help, but there was no one to heed them. The hundreds of comrades all about them were frantically sloshing through the water to save themselves. The roar of battle soon covered up their cries.

The man in front of me was hit and began to float face downward. I made a painful lunge to reach him. As I looked around I saw men everywhere floundering in the water. The waves rolled some of them over on their backs and swept off their helmets. Some of the fallen men were just below the surface of the water, with their equipment weighing them down. When I reached my fallen friend and turned him over on his back I saw that he had been hit in the chest. Grabbing his pack harness, I began to tow him to shore. My woolen clothing was soggily heavy with the cold water. As I barged slowly ahead I suddenly stepped into a hole and sank over my head, losing my grip on my charge. I gasped and swallowed a mouthful of bitter water before I could start to swim. The salty water nearly strangled me. I became panicky and made a wrenching struggle to reach shallow water. When I thought I had reached the other side of the hole I tried to touch bottom, but still it was too deep. The hole must have been gouged out by a large shell from one of the coastal guns. Again I tried for a footing and this time I found the water only knee-deep. While running for shore as fast as I could I looked back at my wounded comrade, floating face down again. I could not go back after him for I was afraid that I could never reach shore with him.

After some time I reached the rocky beach, and there I dropped, exhausted, behind a low cliff. My chest heaved, and I kept choking on the salty slime which had filled my mouth and throat.

I heard someone yelling. When I looked up I saw it was our lieutenant, so I got up and ran over to him. He had organized what was left of our platoon. We moved inland at once between the white tapes which marked a path through the mine fields. I brought up the rear of the tired, water-logged, little band. It numbered only twenty-two now.

We dug into a small field surrounded by hedgerows, and before long our eighty-one-millimeter mortars were barking. It was our first shot at the enemy. The machine guns were set up but quiet.

I went from hole to hole checking on the well-being of each soldier in my platoon. When I came to Lieutenant Sidney, he asked me to check the platoon beside us whose aid man had not made the landing. Everyone seemed to be in good shape, although a few had bruises and scratches.

The chill and darkness of the Normandy night slowly crept upon us. My clothing was still very wet, and I was chilled to the marrow. I looked up at stars which twinkled as brightly here as they did in England or back in the United States. I could even make out the star-outlined dipper. This reminded me of my childhood days, for I still remembered the quiet summer evening on our front porch when, as she held me in her lap, Mother pointed out the Big Dipper to me for the first time and told me an Indian tale about it.

Overhead, clouds gathered, and for awhile it rained, but before long it again cleared, and the stars shone once more. Directly the artillery roared, the skies were lightened by gunshot flashes, and the earth began to shudder. After a thunderous booming it all stopped, and everything was peaceful and quiet again.

At dawn our artillery opened up with a crashing barrage which rocked the whole countryside. When it ceased, we were ordered to move up.

The hedgerows were hazardous to scale. Consisting of earth, small trees, and shrubbery, they were not firm enough to crawl over. The limbs and twigs were not sturdy enough to support one's weight but were large enough and thick enough to prevent one's crawling through them.

After watching several of the others struggle through them, I got a running start, jumped, and plunged over the top of the heaviest of the shrubbery. I landed in a heap on the other side, then regained my feet just in time to see one of the men step on a mine. I walked over to him, cautiously picking my way. His right leg had been blown off at the knee, and the flesh between his knee and crotch was badly mangled. Applying a tourniquet, I wrapped what was left of his leg. While I worked I tried to console him, but his eyes stared out, a picture of naked terror. He told me he was a mechanic from Peru, Indiana, so I told him he'd soon be back there, which was a lot more than many of us could expect. With this he attempted a wry smile and said, "I guess

6

you're right. All I've lost is a leg. Many of you may lose everything."

I put a T of adhesive tape on his forehead and wrote the time the tourniquet was applied.

"They'll pick you up soon," I told him.

I dashed the short distance across a field, found the radioman, and had him give the wounded man's position to the aid station.

Advancing field by field and hedgerow by hedgerow; circling; dodging; hitting the enemy sometimes from the side and other times from the front, even a few times from the rear; walking often two miles to gain fifty yards; this was the pattern of the long days following. Hot, dry, dusty roads by day; dank, rain-soaked, muddy holes by night; so each day passed.

The grass was very thick and long in Normandy and grew from damp, steaming soil which had a very sour stench and gurgled continually, as if fermenting. It was infested with thousands of large, black-and-yellow spotted lizards that slithered into one's pockets and up one's shirt sleeves.

Our line of fighting had been in the form of a large horseshoe, and once again we were headed back toward the sea. From the crest of the hill which we dominated I could see the flashing whitecaps of the distant ocean ahead. I peered cautiously for at the foot of this hill lay a small town buzzing with activity of the enemy preparing for its defense. They outnumbered our outfit three to one and had many large guns and armored vehicles. Now I could see why the defense of the hill was so bitter and determined by the enemy, but this was only a mild preview of what was to happen in our dawn attack.

Under the cover of darkness we advanced to within a stone's throw of the walls of the town, dug two-man foxholes, and took turns at keeping watch. The stillness within the gloomy walls was broken occasionally by the grinding noise that betrayed the advance of a heavy Tiger Royal tank. Each time one began to groan every one of our men automatically stopped breathing for we had learned fear and respect for that seventy-five-ton monster.

I have seen them come out of their stronghold and bear down on the place a rifle platoon had dug in. They would go from hole to hole and machine-gun the occupants to death while they cowered and screamed for mercy. If anyone moved after it had finished, the tank would return to the foxhole, lock one tread, and turn completely around. It would then rumble lazily away, feeling assured that it had ground every soldier into a mass of blood-soaked earth.

As dawn ended the blackness of the long night a devastating artillery barrage descended upon the walled city. The screaming whistle of the falling shells nearly shattered my eardrums. The shots seemed to be barely clearing the large, stone wall before us—a dark, slimy, stinking wall that separated the enemy's watchful eye from mine.

When the artillery stopped the attack order was given. Riflemen began to pour through the gateway in the wall as rifles barked and machine guns rattled.

As our company entered I dashed through the gateway. Just across a small street, facing the gate, was a large

Catholic church. As I rushed toward it to seek shelter in its massive doorway I saw that one of the doors was open wide. Just inside was an enemy machine gun, spitting death into the street and gateway through which I had just run. I squatted in a small corner beside the massive iron hinge of the closed door and stared out into the street.

Several Americans had fallen, and I felt that I must get to them, for some of them must be alive and could be saved. Bullets were flying thickly in all directions, fired from up and down the street, the top of the wall, and house windows. The machine gun in the church was firing across the street, and now someone was returning its fire, for the bullets were passing through the closed door just a few inches from me. My heart sank. Must I be killed by an American bullet?

I was about to dash back into the street when I heard the order to retreat. I cowered in my corner and prayed that I would not be hit by the wild shots of the fleeing soldiers.

When the last American had passed through the gateway in the wall all the firing ceased. I rose and walked boldly into the street.

With their own olive-drab undershirts I covered the faces of the dead. I tried to comfort the dying, and I bandaged the wounds of those who had a chance of living. They lay all about me, very few making a sound.

When I had finished I looked for another American who could help me carry the wounded back to our lines, but the only activity was an occasional enemy soldier scampering across the street. The silence was deathly and unbroken.

9

After I had carried the heavy, wounded men from enemy territory and made them as comfortable as possible in the foxholes we had dug the night before just outside the huge stone wall I sat down to rest. The remainder of the company had dug in a few yards to the right of me. I was perspiring so freely that my clothing was dripping wet. A man just can't dress properly for all occasions in battle. When under fire or engaged in very much activity he practically roasts, but if there is an extended lull and he is lying in a wet hole during a damp night his teeth chatter and his body jerks in convulsions of chill.

The litter bearers had scarcely time to carry off the last wounded man when the artillery again began to fall on the city.

The infantry swarmed over the place, but again they were forced to withdraw. More artillery boomed. Again the infantry surged forward, and again they were pushed out.

It was now later afternoon, and six times we had entered the town, and six times we had been thrown back. Each time I shouldered the burden of removing the wounded. Each time the heavy, limp men had become heavier.

On the last attack we had stayed within that walled town for over an hour but were driven out in a terrific fury of mobilized destruction. Not only were we driven from within the town but clear beyond the strategic hill that we had so gallantly won the day before. The enemy was now dug in on the crest overlooking the hedgerows that concealed what remained of our forces.

I dropped in utter exhaustion against a hedgerow,

my back to the enemy. I wanted to turn away and forget the whole thing. My heart was still pounding and thundering as noisily within my chest as it had since early morning. How much longer could it take it? I felt as if I were dissolved in perspiration, for my body was covered with gritty slime.

I crawled over to a near-by machine gun that had just been set up. The crew had poked a hole through the hedgerow and had put the barrel through it. It afforded excellent protection, but the field of observation was limited.

"Where's Lieutenant Sidney?" I asked.

"He got it in the last attack."

"Dead?"

"Yeah, got it right through the head."

I pondered for a moment and then asked, "Who is in charge?"

The reply was slow. "I am," said the number-one gunner. "Isn't this a hell of a time to get charge of a company?"

We all agreed.

Enemy artillery began to come in, dropping half a dozen shells very close. I hugged the heaving earth, for we had dug no foxholes yet.

When the barrage was over I got to my knees. Two members of the crew did not move, so I rolled them over. They were dead—perforated with shrapnel.

At this moment a terrific hate was born within me. My skin tingled, and my eyes burned red. I now possessed an indescribable hate which will remain with me as long as I live. I had, for the first time, a desire to kill.

I got up behind the machine gun and peered through

the hole in the hedgerow just above the gun sights. I saw two enemy soldiers running in my direction. Quickly, I seized the machine gun and fired two short bursts. They stumbled, grabbed their stomachs, and fell.

Now, I, Frank, a noncombatant medical soldier of the United States, had just committed a crime in violation of an international rule of warfare. I could no longer stand by and watch others kill and be killed. I wanted to fight the common enemy myself.

Cautiously, I crawled through the hedge to my two victims and examined them quite carefully. Each had received several bullets through vital organs. They were quivering, for the last bit of life was ebbing from their bodies. I gazed with amazement. Why had I done it? For a moment I was sorry, terribly sorry, until I remembered that just on the other side of the hedgerow lay two Americans whose bodies were also cooling. I felt almost joyous, bettering the score, but in my mind the score was far from being even, for two Americans are worth a dozen enemy soldiers. I promised myself that I would get more. Perhaps I could even persuade someone to allow me to join the infantry.

As I crawled back through the hedgerow the names of the two enemy soldiers turned over and over in my mind, for they were the first human beings I had ever killed. Otto Trapp and Albert Frey. These names were being etched in my mind as deeply as they were stamped in the round aluminum identification tags which hung from their paling necks.

Soon American fighter planes appeared overhead. They were the first we had seen in two days. They circled momentarily and then swooped down. When midway in the dive, black smoke curled from the front section of each wing. After a few seconds we could hear the roaring chatter of powerful machine guns. Some of the fellows cowered and began to cuss, for they thought they were aiming at us. The planes seemed headed straight for us, but I felt sure that we were safe from it because I had learned to trust the Air Corps.

After each of the planes had swung up from a dive I could hear the Germans yelling. Some were barking orders while others were crying with pain. Again and again the planes returned, and before long even I became nervous. I had witnessed this before, but never had the lines been so close together. The falling, empty cartridges and metal sections of the machine gun belts from the planes clanked loudly upon our helmets.

When the planes stopped diving and hovered overhead the artillery began. After a terrific ten-minute pounding the infantry was ordered to advance—the tired, hungry infantry. The poor, dirty, battered infantry went forward.

As we passed over the crest of that prize hill once again our artillery began roaring. This time it passed on beyond. The planes were dive bombing the town which we had held at brief intervals throughout that day.

Watching all this with awe, I stumbled over the mangled remains of enemy soldiers. I looked around and saw that the area was covered with them. Blood still poured, fresh and red, from their battered bodies. An urge to examine them seized me, but I was carried on by the swift pace toward the little town.

When we entered the smouldering ruins of the little town the bombing and shelling stopped. It made me curious, for even the shells that were coming in from the opposite direction had stopped. Had there been a truce to make even the enemy cease firing? As I looked up and down the rubble-filled streets I heard small-arms fire. I knew now there was no truce.

A few blocks farther on I came upon a dud artillery shell about eight inches in diameter, very smooth and shiny. I looked at it more carefully and then discovered that something had been scratched on its side with a sharp instrument. It was not very legible, but I could make out: "Greetings from the *Tuscaloosa*."

Nightfall found me in much happier mood. I had located a soft bed for the night, had shaved for the first time in several days, and knew that warm food was on its way to us.

I sat down to rest my weary feet, and tears came to my eyes as I thought of how much and how many were behind us in the taking of this small town. We weren't really alone as much as it seemed. It was then that I first realized why it took ten men behind the line to keep one on the line.

With us in the immediate attack of this small town were the Air Corps, artillery, and even the navy with its cruiser, the *Tuscaloosa*. The big brass as well as the little brass did know what was going on, even if those in between were making every day a holiday.

Plenty of chow was delivered to us, because they brought rations for over twice of what was left of the company. I filled my starving insides to capacity. It certainly was satisfying to eat something with a liquid content after surviving on dry K rations for so long.

Before long I felt terribly tired. I told the sergeant where to find me if I were needed, then took a mattress into a basement, and made a bed. I was going to enjoy this night to the fullest extent. The basement would keep out noise as well as protect me from the flying shrapnel that was bound to come throughout the night. I lay down, fully clothed, and fell into a deep sleep almost instantly.

Suddenly I was jolted into consciousness. The orders were to move on again. It seemed that I had just lain down. I looked at my watch—four-thirty.

In a matter of minutes we were filing through the dark, damp streets, passing into the countryside through a battered gateway in the huge wall.

At a chosen spot we dug in. Soon our artillery opened up and was directed a few hundred yards in front of us.

At first I could see our shells exploding around some evenly rounded mounds on a hill. Soon I could make out what they were—the huge emplacements of six long coastal guns pointing out to sea. They could traverse only one hundred and eighty degrees, so we did not fear them. The strategy of our leaders was to attack them from the rear.

The battle was still far from being one sided, however, for many of the enemy we had routed during the past few days were making their final stand. Many mobile field pieces and well-entrenched infantry units could be seen spotting the fields. As soon as they saw us, they brought fire.

Their shells came in and made the earth rave and

heave. They were eighty-eight-millimeter shells. Originally designed as an antiaircraft gun, the eighty-eight had a terrific velocity. Instead of a long and low moaning whistle their shells gave a short, sharp, whistling scream. One had to drop instantly, or all was lost. At such short range the path of the projectile was straight instead of trajectory, thus giving no warning. The shell exploded the instant it was heard.

As my heart pounded we began to move up. More shells came, and I dropped to the ground. A soldier a few yards ahead dropped, rolled over on his back, and lay still. I rushed to his side to give him aid. He appeared unconscious. I knelt down and tried to pick him up to carry him to shelter. As my hands slid beneath him my lower jaw dropped, and I felt faint. My hands had sunk deeply into his chest and abdomen. His entire back had been blown apart. When I withdrew my hands they felt warm and syrupy and were scarlet with congealing blood. I rubbed them in the dirt and grass. What remained I wiped on my trousers which were already spotted with the dried blood of others I had handled the day before.

The enemy was taking a terrible beating. The barren, sandy hill upon which they were entrenched afforded little protection and no concealment. Our artillery and mortar shells rained upon them. Rock and steel flew freely. Occasionally I could see entire gun crews disintegrate in a puff of black smoke. How long could they take it?

A month before I would have had to turn my head on a scene like this, because it would have been too much for me. At this time, however, I looked it squarely in the face and smiled grimly. Every enemy soldier that went down before me meant we were a step closer to the final goal, a step closer to the end. Even hell, with all its conflagration, could be no worse than the slaughter which went on daily before my eyes. It gnawed at my very soul, but now I was a seasoned killer. I no longer flinched when I saw death.

After losing many men as well as equipment, the enemy ceased firing and brought forth white flags. They were ready to surrender. We stayed in our positions and kept our weapons trained upon the enemy, with the exception of one of our men who stood and motioned them to come forward. They came running with their hands high above their heads, waving white pieces of cloth.

We breathed more freely with the fighting over, at least for the time being, and once again we were face to face with the sea.

I walked about and inspected the enemy emplacements. They were well designed, fully equipped, and cleverly concealed. Constructed almost entirely below the surface of the ground, they made a difficult target. Each contained just two openings—an average-sized door in the rear, which was below the ground surface, and a large opening in front for the gun barrel to protrude and traverse. The walls, including those within, were six feet thick, while the roof was about ten feet thick. There were enough shells and supplies to last many months.

The gun itself looked like a huge steam shovel with a massive gun barrel for a boom. On its side was a crane used to load the shells into the breech. I descended an iron ladder into the pit below. The pedestal base upon which this monstrosity rested was carefully marked off in degrees. What a piece of machinery!

As I went through them one by one I came to the last and hesitated. It had received a direct hit in the front opening. The concrete was barely chipped, but the entire gun crew was sprawled about in the disorderly fashion of death. They numbered about fifteen. The stench drove me away.

II.

THE French coast is very alluring. It has the rockiness of Maine with patches of clean, white sand in between. Pretty blue waves dance merrily in, run up the sandy beach, and quickly scamper back again, but its pure, clean, and beautiful appearance was now treacherous. Its clean, white sand was infested with hidden mines. Beautiful waves hid barbed wire and concrete obstacles.

I wandered leisurely through the streets of a small village as the natives straggled in from the near-by woods and hills. Usually the villagers fled when the thunder of war approached for settlements were always the scene of most fighting. As they walked past me they gave a hurried glance of distrust which made me feel unwanted.

Suddenly a middle-aged man came running out of a doorway. His right hand and wrist had been battered and mangled when he had attempted to open a booby-trapped door. Pieces of flesh and blood had splattered his thick, black mustache. As he rushed past I grabbed him. He was startled and showed fear of me, but I pointed to the red cross on my sleeve and motioned for him to lie down. This, he understood. When I had finished dressing his wound, two of our men volunteered to take him to the near-by clinic.

Before I could get away I bandaged a dozen others, sprinkled sulfa powder on children's open sores, and advised expectant mothers. I had used most of the material in my aid kit, given away all my candy, gum, and rations, and had acquired the position of a full-fledged doctor.

When I returned to the company it was late afternoon, and chow had just arrived. It was the first kitchen-prepared food I had seen in the daylight since leaving England.

Nightfall came upon us, the password was issued, and security guards were posted. We bedded down in the bunks formerly used by the enemy crews of the huge coastal guns. It now seemed peaceful and quiet, ever so quiet.

The soft, warm sunshine and fresh, invigorating sea breeze offered a wonderful start for the new day. There was an air of gaiety within the outfit for everyone was whistling and humming. All were busy. Faces were being shaved, socks were being washed, and equipment was being cleaned and oiled. We were issued winter underwear to ward off the chill of the damp Normandy night.

Replacements arrived—nice, clean, fresh replacements. They looked young and shiny beside the others but two weeks hence they would look as hard and weary as any veteran. Their uniforms were neat and clean, and they fitted well. There were sharp creases in their trousers, and their field jackets were bright and new. They carried a full pack of extra equipment. The extra shoes, socks, and underwear would come in very handy. Most of the boys got very chummy with a replacement about their size, in anticipation of getting a few badly needed new clothes.

I managed to get a new pair of trousers to replace the dirty ones that I had worn since England. Those blood-spotted trousers had sentimental value, because they had been through so much. The dirty, baggy trousers had gotten creases behind the knees after the regular creases disappeared while wading ashore. But, all in all, I was glad to get rid of those grimy trousers with their rasping roughness and the disagreeable odor of the gas repellent they had been saturated with in England.

As evening came once again we were fed. An ordnance man checked all weapons, repaired any that were not up to standard, and returned with the jeep that brought chow.

A convoy of trucks, driven by French civilians, arrived. We were loaded in, warned to keep all lights out, and started off down a rough side road.

One can always tell a new replacement, even in the dark. He talks. The seasoned fighter sits quietly and stares into space. He does not smile nor even laugh at the funniest of jokes.

The ride was a jolting one, even rougher than necessary. These Frenchmen couldn't have driven a wheelbarrow properly. They hit every hole in the road, drove in ditches, and ran over the curbs. Only an American six-by-six could take it without breaking down or getting stuck. Here were the finest trucks in the world, but not enough Americans were yet ashore to drive them.

Some griped about the situation, but most of us understood. If the government had not hired these Frenchmen, we would have walked. The fellows all meant well, even if it did get a bit unbearable at times. I only hoped nothing too drastic would happen, for if I were to die I was determined to die of enemy action and not from an accident.

We came up to our own artillery lines, unloaded, and let the trucks go back.

A near-by howitzer, which had been so cleverly camouflaged that most of us had not seen it, fired a round and sent some of the new men into a fit of fear. Some fell to the ground, while others ran, but most of them were grabbed by a seasoned veteran and told not to get excited, that we were still a couple of miles from the front. The new men felt much better. No one had told them where they were. Some had thought they were at the front, others that they might be behind enemy lines, while still others thought it was the explosion of an incoming shell.

They did not understand the lineup and order of battle as we did. A soldier who is familiar with combat routine can easily keep track of his location, especially if there is much activity. At first one hears the distant thunder and can see the lightning-like flashes of his own artillery. As it is approached, the same signs of the enemy artillery appear a few miles farther on. Somewhere in between, the infantry of each side must be in contact. Sometimes, during a lull in the fighting, it may become difficult to figure out these things easily, but a bit of quiet, careful observation will usually tell one.

We moved up on line and dug in. It was rather quiet, with the exception of an occasional shell crashing in the near-by woods. Our mortars fired now and then to keep the enemy awake and aware of our presence. Being set up only a few feet away and making a very distinctive "pung" when fired, they also kept me awake.

Our artillery seemed to increase its pace with the coming of dawn. It was landing far ahead, however.

We pulled out and filed down a narrow, dusty road. After covering half a mile without incident we were fired upon. No one was hit, and our troops quickly deployed in so orderly a fashion that it amazed me how well the replacements behaved.

We moved up a few hedgerows, extremely close together here. My machine gun section moved up on line with the riflemen, and occasionally bayonet fighting broke out. The enemy was firing very freely, much too freely, but the bullets did not pass through the trees the way they used to.

Soon I found the answer. One of the fellows had been hit in the upper part of his left arm. Instead of shattering the bone and passing on through, the bullet itself shattered when it hit the bone. It was made of wood! What a mess! The single, clean-cut hole that I was used to was much better to dress than this. The entire portion of the upper arm was filled with splinters; even the left side of his body was full of them. I pulled as many out as I could, but most of them were buried too deeply and caused too much pain. How I wished

23

they would have used just plain steel bullets. The wood had been treated with some solution that gave it a lavender color; it must have been poisonous, judging from the pain that it caused.

I went from man to man, warning each about the wooden splinters from the bullets. He might be able to ward off the flying ones if he knew that the bullets were made of wood and understood that they shattered on hitting a tree or rock. Several of the fellows already had pieces of the bullets in their faces and hands. I tried to remove them, but it was almost impossible because I had only a pocketknife. They were so deeply embedded and broke off so easily that I decided to leave them alone. Most of them were not serious enough to put a man out of action but were quite painful and annoying. A splinter in the cheek or forehead caused profuse watering of the eyes.

I saw another who had just been hit in the upper part of his left arm. He toppled over and appeared unconscious. When I looked him over more closely I saw that he was dead. A splinter had gone through his arm and had pierced his heart.

The fighting was very close. It had to be to use wooden bullets for they would not carry far. Hand grenades spread a pall of black smoke over us.

Two prisoners had been taken. After they were searched I crawled over to them and asked why they were using wooden bullets. They seemed rather ignorant, each giving a different answer. One said it was practice ammunition used on the manuevers held just before the invasion and that it worked well in close fighting. The other contradicted him by saying that they were used only in the machine guns, that every tenth shell fired a wooden bullet to clean the barrel.

Before long the artillery was pelted upon the enemy in great quantity. I saw one shell make a direct hit on the camouflaged setup used by the enemy's forward observer, an artilleryman who goes along with infantry. Usually picking a high place for observation from which he could direct the artillery, he had a telephone or radio over which he contacted the gun crews with information as to good targets and reported where each shell landed until they made a hit. Once he told them they had hit within the target area, they would train all guns on it and usually blow the whole place up. He was the one who spied upon us, trained those huge guns on us, and made us feel and see a living hell. He made the earth heave and shudder. He made my comrades disappear in the soil. Now his long, white underwear hung in shreds in a near-by tree—a symbol of his surrender. The motorcycle he used for traveling and carrying his equipment was scattered about.

The artillery ceased, and we moved up. A few prisoners were taken, but the main body of the enemy had made a successful retreat.

A small enemy plane appeared overhead and flew lazily in large circles. Some of the fellows fired at it, but it was a difficult target. Soon shells began to fall upon us for the plane had replaced the artillery observer that we had so recently killed.

We moved swiftly out under cover of the trees and shrubs. The observer in the plane had not seen us, so thinking we were still in the old spot, he continued to have the shells rain upon it.

A wooded location always presents a difficult problem. It is dark and dangerous, and the field of vision is very limited. The animals that inhabit it often startle one, cause confusion, and sometimes bring unwanted shooting. Even the wind is against an attacking force.

As we entered this grove of evergreens, a hail of bullets greeted us. It turned out to be only a handful of soldiers who surrendered after a brief but heated battle.

We moved swiftly but cautiously ahead, for it was late afternoon. We wanted to clear the woods before daylight slipped away.

Just before we mopped up the woods, we came upon a sickening sight. Several paratroopers were hanging in the trees. Apparently they had tried to hit the open field which lay just ahead of us. Their camouflaged parachutes were tangled in the treetops, and they hung, limp, battered, and decaying, by their shroud lines. As we came closer it was apparent that they had been victims of foul play. Those hanging high were literally riddled with bullet holes, while those hanging lower had been subjected to a merciless bayoneting. The intestines of some hung to the ground, while others had been completely disemboweled. A few had been disrobed, and portions of their bodies were missing. Nearly all had been relieved of their shoes.

Once again I was burning inside, glowing for revenge. The terrific hate which I had so recently acquired made my teeth grind and my fists clench. If given a chance, I would stop at nothing, for my mind was now well conditioned for combat. If every fighting man felt as I did, this would be the most brutal war conceivable. Everyone and everything that gave the slightest evidence of

26

unfriendliness would be beaten and battered beyond recognition.

Dawn came once again, and the artillery barrage had as its objective another small town.

Suddenly an American soldier came running from enemy territory. He was treated as a captured enemy until he proved his identification. His beard was long, his face dirty, and his clothing tattered and torn. He was a paratrooper who had been lost from his organization and had been hiding behind the enemy lines. He would have tried to join us during the night but was afraid of being shot by our sentries. I gave him two of my K rations. Quickly he gobbled them up.

The lieutenant gave him a weapon, some ammunition, and a few hand grenades. Our outfit was grateful to have gained an experienced fighter, and this veteran was very happy to have joined an experienced outfit.

We entered the town and gradually fought on. As the battle raged through it, we came upon an enemy machine gun set up at the main intersection. It give us considerable trouble.

Suddenly, out of the corner building, rushed an American firing a small automatic weapon. It was our paratrooper. He had picked up an enemy machine-pistol, and was now using it on them. The machine gun was knocked out of action. He had killed or wounded the entire crew. What a feat!

Though the town was cleared of the enemy we were soon plagued with snipers. They seemed to be of the spirit type. We would surround and enter the house from which they fired and then search it from the basement to the rooftop, but all we could find were the civilians who inhabited it.

Finally, one of the fellows managed to hit one of the snipers firing from an upstairs window. The house was rushed, and a young French woman was dragged out. She had been wounded.

One of the Americans, who spoke French fluently, questioned her. She had been married to a German for four years and had two children by him. Now he was dead—killed fighting the Americans. She was very bitter toward the Americans. Could we really blame her? Several other snipers turned out to be the same kind.

Her rifle was broken, and she was turned over to the French constable of the town.

Many of the girls who had, at one time or another, associated with the Germans, were rounded up and taken to the public square in the center of town. There they had their hair cut off and their heads shaved. This seemed to be a very harsh treatment, for it brought great humiliation and made them social outcasts throughout the nation. It would take at least one, perhaps two, years for their hair to grow long. Until that time, they would have an unforgettably trying time in their newly liberated country.

We pushed on. Hedgerow after hedgerow, field after field, town after town. How long had we been at it? I did not know. Hours, days, weeks, years. I no longer measured time in that manner. I just knew that certain incidents happened so many towns back or when Charlie or Joe was with us.

It seemed an endless task. Regardless of what happened, the general pattern was the same. A few days before, the enemy forward observer got hit, but within fifteen minutes he was replaced with one in an airplane. Soldiers by the dozens fell before us, but still there were dozens, hundreds, thousands more. They still presented a solid front before us. Again and again we had stormed towns and villages. Settlement after settlement we had captured, only to find another lying over the next hill.

For three days we had been stalled, for the enemy had massed great forces in such a manner as to stop us completely. Apparently the entire front was at a standstill, just sitting back and slugging it out with artillery.

Three times we had tried to penetrate, but each time we were met with such force that it had been given up, at least for the time being. Now only the artillery and Air Corps had duels. Occasionally we got a good pounding from artillery, but it was not as often as we had been used to. We watched the fighter planes fight it out, often making small bets on them. They were always so high that it became difficult to watch them in the bright, shiny atmosphere.

We were told that we could write a letter home. This was the first chance in a long time. We could write but one letter, for all letters must be censored. Each must be carefully read by our officer. Since he was right with us, and just as busy as we, he did not have time to read very many. He asked us to write very simply and in as few words as possible.

I was much more fortunate than many of the others, for I had a pencil. It had been issued to me to fill out the emergency medical tags that I fastened to each soldier to whom I gave aid. My next problem was to find paper and an envelope. All of my stationery, as well as two

29

dollars' worth of air-mail stamps, were ruined when I waded ashore.

I crawled from hole to hole, asking each fellow if he had any stationery to spare. I had learned not to bother the old members of the company, for I knew they were even more unfortunate than I—they had no pencil. I finally came onto a new replacement who had a few V-mail forms in his gas mask carrier. He told me to take all of them, for he had no one to write to. I talked him into keeping one in case he should think of someone. Of the remainder, I kept one and distributed the rest to the boys in the holes that I passed on my way back. Each made some humorous remark about playing mailman or delivering unwritten mail.

I settled as comfortably as possible in my foxhole, and tried hard to write a nice letter to my mother, but I did not know what to write. I could not write about our activity or the weather because it was a military secret. Many of our military moves were based upon the weather or weather reports. There were many events and incidents that happened daily, but she wouldn't want to know about them—I wouldn't want her to.

I wrote about ten lines in the letter, mostly questions asking how things were going at home. I let her know that I was still in good health. I knew that if she could have seen me as I looked she would have rushed me to a hospital. I did not want her or any other mother to know how we looked or what we were going through.

Many of the tanks had been outfitted with a scoop affair in front which operated much like a bulldozer, so we called them tankdozers. They worked very well in the hedgerows. It was much easier to dash through the gaping holes they made than to struggle through the dense growth.

Like any other tank they drew a great amount of artillery fire. Some of the fellows compared the tank with a woman—you cannot live with one or without one. When the enemy saw, or even suspected, a tank of being in the vicinity, they tried to hit it with an artillery shell. This usually made the infantrymen around it sweat and pray and cuss, but at the same time they knew that they wouldn't want to be left without one. Its heavy armor, nimble machine guns, and powerful cannon had often put the odds on our side when stiff resistance was encountered. I had seen them knock many a sniper out of a church steeple or other tower who could have caused us more casualties and held us up much longer.

A group of heavy bombers appeared above us. Many of them had passed over us bombing the industrial centers and great rail centers which lay a few hundred miles ahead. Often I had wondered what it would be like to fight our way into a large city. Would it be better or worse than the close fighting in the fields and small villages? Suddenly the fellow beside me told me to look up. The planes did not pass over, but turned to our right and disappeared.

Soon there was a thin line of smoke passing by just in front of us. Smoke pots had been set out at various intervals along the line, and a gentle breeze was blowing the smoke slowly, but precisely, between the two battle lines.

Suddenly a roaring thunder broke loose about a mile away. After a short interval, I could see what was taking place. The heavy bombers that had just passed were returning and dropping their load as they came. They were bombing the installations, entrenchments, and fortifications of the enemy. Their guide was the column of smoke passing between the enemy and us.

The planes continued to pass over before us. There were many times the number that had passed by at first. The enemy was taking a terrific pounding, for the amount and color of the black smoke from the bombs rising high in the clean blue sky were evidence that the bombs were hitting many of their targets.

After a time I became nervous. I had never imagined such powerful mass destruction, such ruin on so large a scale. I was thankful that we were not on the receiving end of it. I thought of what kept us from it—that column of smoke, just that thin line of smoke. I shuddered to think of what would happen if anything went wrong with it.

I watched the bombers pass over, wave after wave. The huge four-engined monsters flying so gracefully appeared unafraid of the antiaircraft fire that exploded all about them.

At first they ploughed through the air. Their tails were a bit low and the shiny noses pointed slightly upward. They were trying to climb with their heavy burden. As they released their load, their engines roared a sigh of relief, the tails became level again, and the noses pointed forward.

When suddenly the wind changed the impossible happened. The smoke was being blown directly over our line. I prayed that it would go no farther, that it would not pass on behind us.

But my prayers were in vain, for soon the smoke was

behind us. A lump came to my throat, and I swallowed hard to make it disappear. Maybe it would have been better to have broken the enemy line without the aid of the Air Corps. Perhaps it would have been less costly to have used the ground forces alone. I am sure, that if given another chance, the infantrymen of this sector would rather have tried it than face what was about to happen, for soon the ground began to pitch and boom. The bombardment was on. Great geysers of earth spouted up, huge craters appeared, erupting large clods of earth.

Another soldier jumped into my hole. I did not know him. We cowered in my small foxhole, but it was no protection. Pieces of earth, rock, and trees rained upon us. I looked at my friend, and he looked at me and spoke. I heard nothing, so I put my head close to his mouth. He yelled into my ear. I felt the force of his breath upon my eardrums, but still I heard nothing.

I began to wonder how long it would be before they stopped. How long would it be before they found out that they were bombing their own troops? Couldn't the artillerymen see this? Couldn't they radio the planes?

Then I thought that perhaps someone had radioed them, but they would not stop until they were sure that it was not a trick—a message sent by the enemy.

Many thoughts passed through my mind. I tried to think of some better means of protection. Even if the hole were deeper, it would not have helped. I looked up at the mound of earth that I had shoveled out when I made the hole and felt like pulling it in upon me. Anything, anything at all, to protect me from the powerful blasts.

33

A bomb landed very close. The force was terrific. It felt as if my belt had been pulled up so tight that the ends of the buckle met, that my waist measurement was less than an inch. My mouth was open and my tongue seemed to have been pushed completely out of my throat and mouth. As this blast of air passed beyond, it was followed by somewhat of a moment of vacuum. Then my stomach flew out beyond even its original boundaries, and my tongue snapped back into my throat. All of this within a fraction of a second.

I shook the dirt from myself. My stomach was burning, and I felt weak. Perhaps my insides had been shaken loose. I looked for my friend. He was lying partly out of the hole. His eyes had been torn from their sockets. One lay on his cheek, while the other had been disconnected and was gone completely. His death had been caused by a ruptured bladder. He had forgotten or neglected what he had been told so many times—to urinate often. A full bladder is very easily broken by concussion.

The bombardment stopped, but still I was afraid to peer out. What I had just experienced was beyond conception. The spark of life still remained within me, and now, more than ever before, I wished to retain it.

Once again I remembered my duty, so I got out of the hole and looked about. A pall of smoke and dust hung over the sector. Now again the enemy was getting the full force of the bombardment. I pulled my unknown comrade the rest of the way out of the hole, laid him on the ground, and covered his face. Then I went about in search of the wounded.

A surprisingly small number had been wounded. Most of the casualties were suffering from some sort of

34

concussion or were dead. Several of those killed need not have been, if they had only remembered their training lectures.

A new replacement suffered a broken neck. He had fastened his helmet strap under his chin, and the force of onrushing air of a near-by explosion created a terrific jerk on his helmet. If he had let the strap hang or had fastened it around the back of his helmet, he might still have been alive.

This gave me the idea that I could save others from this same fate. I checked on each man to see how he fastened his helmet, and when I came across any doubtful case I showed him mine.

The strap on my helmet had been cut off completely, and the steel was dented in a few places to keep it from falling off the plastic liner beneath it. I had adjusted the leather strap of the liner so that it fit just beneath the knowledge bump on the back of my head. This kept it from falling off when I had to hit the ground fast.

Once again we were off on an attack upon the enemy. This was a large-scale attack, for there were more tanks being used than I had ever seen massed before. Along the entire front the artillery rumbled and roared.

Our Company D, Dog Company, was to support the leading attack company. In this case it was Company C, the Charlie Company.

Each company bore the name of a letter of the alphabet. To keep them from being confused on the radio or telephone, a word was substituted for the letter. Our battalion consisted of four companies, A, B, C, and D, or Able, Baker, Charlie, and Dog. The first three were rifle companies, and we of Dog Company were the heavy machine gun and mortar company.

As we moved up, the fighting became more intense. The enemy still had plenty of fight.

We were closing in on a hilltop town. The enemy was well protected and heavily fortified within its walls. As we approached we were forced to advance across a large open field without protection. The enemy stared down our very throats.

Machine guns raked the area. Their crossfire was very deadly. Soon the eighty-eights from an antiaircraft position had been leveled upon us and fired point blank. It gave no warning that way. They made two booming roars connected by a whistling scream. The first explosion was the bursting of the projectile. A split second later, one could hear the boom as the shell left the barrel and traveled faster than sound.

The riflemen advancing just ahead of us were being thinned out very rapidly. There were gaping holes in their formation, and before long they were all but annihilated. The scattered few who remained fell and hoped that they would be spared. We were forced to run back and the enemy stomped after us. We organized a defense which stopped them and then drove them back within the town.

Once again we were organized and prepared to make another assault upon the town. This time we were to support Baker Company, which was to lead the attack. Once again we were beaten to our knees and forced to withdraw.

A truce had been declared for two hours. During this time both sides were to remove the dead and wounded.

Most of our casualties lay in no man's land. I went out to give what aid I could. Men lay in great numbers, and the ground was pitted with craters freshly made by shrapnel—the shiny, gray pieces of steel that tear huge holes in human tissue.

The enemy medical aid men were busy in the same locality. Their helmets were enameled a glossy white, and a large white bib, the width of their bodies, hung to their knees in both front and back. It had a huge red cross in the center, making them difficult to mistake for a fighting soldier.

I knelt beside an American and bandaged the calf of his right leg where a bullet had passed completely through. About six feet away lay a wounded German soldier who had been struck in the chest. He moaned and gurgled.

A German medical soldier came to him. Kneeling, he examined the wounded man's chest. Using his fingers, he opened the man's eye and examined it closely. He shook his head in a negative manner, as if to indicate that there was no hope. Reaching into his first-aid kit, he withdrew a shiny, small-caliber revolver. He cocked it and then fired into the wounded man's head. The man suddenly stiffened but gradually relaxed. He was dead.

Even as the aid man walked away I continued to gape at him. This action had temporarily stunned me. What a method of mercy!

I walked back and joined the company again. They were all well dug in. I looked at my badly blistered hands. Must I dig another hole?

A voice called to me, "Hey, Doc! Come on over and join me."

37

It was the paratrooper we had picked up a few days before, so I scurried over and jumped in beside him.

The sky was clear and blue and the air fresh and clean. The quiet stillness seemed wonderful. I inhaled deeply. It felt magnificent not to be hunted or preyed upon. Around the foxhole the bright red poppies swayed gently to and fro in the breeze. This beautiful wild flower, destroyed as a weed, so different from any I had seen in America, recalled a poem written by a soldier in the last war. Then I remembered what happened to him.

I looked at my friend and found that he was staring into space—all wrapped up in thought thousands of miles away. I broke the silence, "How long have you been a paratrooper?"

"About a year and a half," he answered.

"Made many jumps?"

"Hell no. Never jumped once, but I've been pushed seventeen times. You know, I've been thinking. I've been a snafu ever since I joined. Even on this jump into Normandy, I got lost from my outfit. Never did find them. It's lucky I bumped into you fellows. If I hadn't I'd probably be cold turkey by now. You know, for the last couple of days I've been thinking that my number's just about up."

"Don't talk that way." I looked into his young kid face, just aged with war. "Don't talk like a fool, Joe."

"Well, I haven't told anyone else, but it just came to me the other day. Probably just another one of those crazy ideas of mine."

Several times I had seen or heard this same thing. Often their intuition turned out to be correct. Perhaps

38

God had sent them a spiritual message to give them time to become prepared.

A shell came whistling in, telling us that the truce was over. Circling dive bombers were working the town over as our artillery began to rake the enemy positions. We were back at the old game.

The town was stormed again. This time the eighty-eights did not interfere, for they had been knocked out of action. The small-arms fire was quite intense, but soon it all but ceased. The enemy soldiers saw their helpless position and either fled or surrendered. They had never faced such an onslaught of tanks and armor before.

The street fighting was quite difficult. Our soldiers found that they must advance up the streets in nearly every case. Ordinarily, when they ran into stiff resistance, they went up the alleys and across the back yards.

In this place nearly every yard had a stone wall about seven feet high, and along the top, imbedded in the concrete, were hundreds of sharp pieces of broken glass. These protruded in such a manner as to make it impossible to scale the wall without being cut very severely.

It was after dark by the time the last shot was fired. Hot chow was brought up and since it was the first in several days we ate a good stomachful.

I looked for a good house to sleep in, but it was impossible to find one, for they had all been smashed. Most of the houses were made of mud and sticks and one shell was enough to tear them apart. What remained standing was very dangerous to live in. A good wind or rain storm could possibly level the remainder of the town.

I found a large, empty wine cask, rolled it into a

bomb crater, and knocked out half of one end. After finding some straw I crawled in and went to sleep.

That night I dreamed of the American officer who lay in state in the heart of the town into which he had tried to lead his men. He was killed in the attack, but was carried in by the men he commanded. On this day he was known as the Major of St. Lo.

III.

ONCE again we moved on. On again in hot pursuit of the fleeing enemy. They could have moved much faster if they were only trying to flee, but they were trying to take as much of their equipment as possible. They destroyed whatever they could not take with them, leaving nothing of any value.

Their fight of delayed action did not work so well, for the mines they planted had been buried too quickly, making them easily detected in the newly turned earth. We came across several in shallow holes that had not even been covered.

Many of the trees beside the road had been prepared as very efficient road blocks by tying small bricks of high explosive around each of them. Our scouts clipped the wires which linked the trees together. Sometimes we found them so near completion that the detonating mechanism had been placed at the ends of the wires. They needed only to be connected to set off the charge.

This was proof that we were at the enemy's heels. At times we could even hear the commotion caused by some confusion in their flight.

For the next days the pursuit continued, fifteen, eighteen, and twenty miles a day. The terrain was quite level, but even under ideal conditions this fast pace was

41

too much. It was starting to show on the haggard-looking soldiers, who no longer even looked for loot. With their whiskers long and their faces dirty, they very seldom attempted to clean up, for every spare moment was given to relaxation. When they sat or lay down, they fell asleep almost immediately. This type of warfare may have been designed for mechanized units, but it was too much for a foot soldier.

Late one evening, after a long day of hard going, we held up in a small French village. There we were told that we would remain for the time being—perhaps a day or two. The rapid progress of the past few days had stretched the lines of supply to a near breaking point. It would have been disastrous had the enemy reorganized and counter attacked.

We occupied a small barracks which had been used by the German soldiers. Doubledecked wooden bunk beds with straw-filled mattresses, good wooden floors, and a tile roof over our heads to keep us from the outside elements made it seem like a heaven to us. We even had showers with plenty of running water.

Most American civilians would have shied away from a place like this, for it was crude and dingy looking. But to the infantry, the boys who knew what rough going was like, it was a wonderful place. A chance to bathe, to shave and clean up, to change socks and wash the sweaty underwear that had been clinging to the body for several weeks, made them look and feel a hundred per cent better—more like human beings than animals.

During the next day those who did not stand guard had a very enjoyable time lounging around. We had to stay inside or under cover as much as possible, for if the enemy were allowed to see very many troops they would have guessed that at least a company was here. This might have brought some heavy shelling.

The French civilians were more friendly in this sector than those near the coast. They freely gave us much valuable information about the enemy. Apparently they had been treated much more harshly. Many things had been taken from them, and their rations had not been ample. The food supply was very low. Perhaps the Germans had favored the Normans on the coast to gain their aid in the case of an invasion.

We took turns giving each other haircuts. Most of the older men of the company got theirs cut very short. Some even shaved their heads. I got mine shaved because it was much easier to wash a bare head, and I found that it must be washed frequently for the dust, dirt, and perspiration made my scalp itch and feel lousy.

Most of the new replacements who had just arrived shied away from these short haircuts. I tried to talk them into getting one for I knew it would be much better for them, but they chuckled at my naked-looking head, and gave me a polite "We'll see." I tried to shame them into it by telling them that they were fighting men, that their lives were the most important things over here, that furloughs didn't exist, and they would soon forget playing Romeo. They still refused.

During the evening half a dozen tanks crept into the village. Our infantry division was going to team up with an armored division, and together we would chase the enemy over the moors, through the forests, and back within his original boundaries. At least that was what we were told.

Early the next morning we started the chase across northern France. We moved very rapidly, and almost unmolested. The speed was so great that very little walking could be done. Most of the fellows rode on tanks, trucks, and even in captured vehicles.

I found a bicycle which I rode for nearly two days. During the end of the second day, however, I was forced to abandon it. While approaching a small village, we were fired upon. The battle which followed made me crawl in ditches and gutters, go through back yards, and dash from house to house.

Soon the fight was over, and we moved out of the village on a narrow dirty road. I was riding on the top of a tank. The driver had his hatch open and his head sticking out. This made driving a bit easier for him, for his range of vision was nearly unlimited. While inside a tank, he had to look through a narrow opening. The interior also got quite hot after a long run on a warm day.

The road was of dirt and the tanks made so much dust that it turned our clothes a light tan.

Occasionally the tank driver looked up, gave me a huge smile, and winked as if to say, "How are we doing?" or "Don't we make a wonderful team?" His face was full of powdery dust. The dark whiskers and eyebrows were now blond. I could see the grains of sand in his ears. He had goggles on his forehead, for they became dirty too quickly to be used. The wrinkles and creases on his forehead and face were very dark and vivid. There the dust had been saturated with sweat, which made it dark and muddy. His eyelashes were dust laden, and the white portion of the watering eyeballs were a dark pink, agitated by the sand and grit. The corners of his eyes were black with the dirt that had collected there, and riding along the edge of his lower eyelid was a dark rim of the same gritty substance.

When he looked around again, I noticed how white and bright-looking his teeth were. I looked around at the white teeth of the others. Unconsciously, I ran my tongue over my teeth and found my mouth full of a very fine abrasive substance—that dust! Over a short period of time it had accumulated in everyone's nose and mouth, making even the dullest teeth sparkle after a very short time.

While passing through a small town we were fired upon by a lone sniper. One of the fellows got hit in the chest and fell instantly, letting out a long, low moan, as if he had the wind knocked out of him.

Quickly I pulled him out of the street so a passing tank would not run over him. Their field of vision was very limited, for they had closed all their hatches, or "buttoned up," as we called it.

About three buildings up the street was a fair-sized hotel. I decided to take my wounded companion into it for comfort, as well as protection.

As I went through the door I could hear the firing growing more intense. Howitzers were being used. I decided to take him down into the basement. The hotel was a brick structure, but I wanted to be doubly safe, rather than doubly sorry. I didn't want a wounded companion killed or even wounded again unnecessarily.

Once in the basement I placed him on the floor. With bandage scissors I cut a large opening in the clothing around his wound. The hole in his chest was about the size of a dime. The bullet had lodged in his chest for it

45

had not passed through. He must have been in great pain, for his eyes rolled about in their sockets as if caused by spasm. The wound was clean, but it had punctured a lung, making the air wheeze and form large bubbles in the oozing blood.

I bandaged it very tightly, but still air was being sucked in when he inhaled. I folded my raincoat into a small, compact square and placed it over the bandage. Removing the belt from the wounded man's trousers, I placed it around his chest and over the raincoat, fastening it securely and just tight enough to stop the air. That was the most I could do. Then the blood began to bubble from his nose and mouth.

Before long I brought in two other wounded soldiers whose conditions were less serious than the first. By the time I had finished with the last, the litter bearers arrived and took all three of them away from the hazards of the front to the safety of the rear.

For each man I saw go back like that, I breathed a little prayer for his safety on the way. He had seen enough. He had done his part in this war, and had given one of his most prized possessions—blood, perhaps even his life. I had heard of several cases where they had been hit by a stray bullet or caught in an artillery barrage on the way back. I hoped that, if I must ever go back, that the war would be over, or that I would be unconscious. I did not want to pass through the dead space between our infantry and our artillery in a helpless manner. It was a treacherous piece of territory, and, aside from no man's land, it was the most lifeless place I knew.

In the basement room of the hotel was a good-sized safe. It had aroused my curiosity since I first entered this place, but I was too busy to bother with it. Now I had a few free moments and wanted to see what was inside.

I examined it carefully to see if it was booby trapped. It appeared free of wires, so I tried the handle. Just as I had expected—it was locked. This did not stop me.

After a short search through the town, I located a soldier with a bazooka (rocket launcher). I made a proposition with him whereby he was to get half of the loot.

We got back to the hotel, and I showed him the safe just opposite the basement window—a perfect shot.

The foundation of the hotel was of heavy rock, so it afforded good protection from the blast. We knocked the glass from the window. Kneeling at one side, he aimed the launcher, then, pulling his head away so that the foundation protected him, he fired the weapon. There was a deafening explosion.

We waited a moment for the dust and smoke to clear before we went into the basement. The door of the safe had been nearly torn off, and there was paper lying all about the room—negotiable paper—French currency. Much of it had been burned or torn. A few pieces of women's jewelry lay about, but they were badly battered. A man's gold pocket watch had been broken to bits. We picked up all the undamaged currency, for it might have come in handy should we get a pass or go back for a rest. We had no money of our own since we hadn't been paid since leaving England.

We gathered up approximately two thousand dollars in French francs. After splitting it, the bazooka man left.

47

The bills varied from one-thousand to two-franc notes. They varied in size accordingly, the largest the size of an eight-by-ten diploma. The variations in size made it a very unmanageable roll of paper, but I jammed it into my shirt pocket and dashed off in search of my outfit.

The opposition had been overcome and we moved on again. Kilometer after kilometer, town after town. Occasionally we ran into opposition, but it was readily overcome. The resistance of the enemy was very feeble and unorganized. It was a full-scale rout, for the enemy was fleeing and surrendering very rapidly.

For the last few days we had been headed for Paris, but we turned north again. Some other outfit was to get the credit for freeing it. I really wish that we could.

Up to the time that we were on an even line with Paris I had hoped that perhaps we would turn south and get the honors of liberating it. But we raced past the gay city and on toward the enemy homeland—on to the thick forests, the dark hills, and the heavily fortified concrete pillboxes.

There were rumors of peace. Of course, we knew nothing but what we heard; all news was by word of mouth. Many were cheerful and thought the news would break momentarily, but most of us were more skeptical, although very hopeful. The enemy had been on the run for several weeks, and perhaps they would make a peace offer before we entered their homeland. Some of the boys remembered the rout in Africa which led to our eventual victory there.

As the discussion got under way, a few arguments broke out. Silence came over the group as some of the

48

older men of the company expressed their opinions. They had been at this business of war for a long time, and had been taking part in this flight for the past weeks. Yes, they remembered the rout in Africa—all too well. They also recalled that we were slowed down occasionally by enemy equipment—not just because it was used on us, but because it very often blocked the way. When the Germans fled in Africa, they left mountains of equipment scattered along the way. When they were finally cornered, they didn't just surrender. They fought a gallant battle. They beat us back several times, and cost us many casualties. Even with all the men and equipment they lost, they still offered us a mighty bout.

Here, since the break-through at St. Lo, the retreat of the enemy had been orderly. They had not lost a great number of their men and had retained most of their equipment. Somewhere, someday, we would run onto it.

One evening, we had to clear one more wooded hill to make sure of our security before we held up for the night. It was one of those hot, lazy summer evenings when the aroma of the woodland is so enticing. The pollen of wild flowers was stimulating to my nostrils. I breathed it deeply and drank in the scenery. It was a calm, peaceful place, and the small hill looked lonesome and innocent; even the trees seemed to be too young to be holding anything treacherous. As we wound our way up a narrow footpath a few playful insects flitted past my face, and a lone deer scampered into the thicket at our side. No human being could be anywhere about.

When the lead scout came to the crest of the hill, he signaled for everyone to get down. There were Germans

49

ahead, and we had to rout them this evening to be secure for the night.

Everyone crawled up on line. Being curious, I crawled up for a ringside seat.

The enemy did not know that we were near. They apparently had cleared the hill before and now thought they were safe for the night for no guards were posted. It was a very strict rule with the American army that if only two soldiers were stationed on a tiny island a thousand miles from anywhere, one would be standing guard while the other slept.

They were preparing their supper, and a side of beef hung in a near-by tree. Two of the soldiers were tending to the cooking over a small fire, while another, sitting propped against a tree, was playing a harmonica. It certainly was a cozy, unsuspecting party.

A machine gun had been silently set up just to my right. All the others were ready with their particular weapons, ready if they should be needed. I could even see a second machine gun poised without its tripod.

The lieutenant let forth with a yell. He yelled, in the few German words he knew, for them to halt, and to come with their hands up.

The harmonica playing stopped abruptly. The silence was nerve racking. One by one the surprised enemy dropped what was in his hands and raised them above his head. An indescribable look of amazement covered each face.

A few of our fellows with small weapons got up and started toward them. The Germans stood perfectly still with their hands upraised.

Suddenly I noticed one lone enemy soldier, standing

in the shadows of the background, who had a machine-pistol in his hands. It was pointed in our direction.

This machine-pistol was a type of submachine gun with a retractable wire stock. It fired a nine-millimeter shell—about the same as our thirty-eight-caliber pistol ammunition. They were used very extensively in Normandy. It looked like a submachine gun used by the paratroopers.

I tried to yell a cry of warning, but no sound would come forth. The gun burst out with a smooth, quiet, ripping sound; somewhat like the sound of canvas being torn so that most of the fellows referred to them as "burp guns." The soldiers before me dropped to the ground. No one had been hit. Still the machine-pistol purred on. It swept over us once without incident, but as it arched back over us again, it found its mark. I seemed to be in the center of the arc it struck, for the two men on the left felt its sting. It seemed to hold its mark on the fellow to my left. He cried out. He yelled for mercy, for forgiveness, for God, and finally, for his mother. As the bullets jerked into his already convulsing body, the machine gun on my right barked out. Its slow, determined rattle knocked the die-hard enemy soldier over.

The fight was over; the hill was secured.

As the other soldiers cautiously converged on the former enemy encampment, I dressed the wounds of the remaining two soldiers. One had been hit once in the arm, the other had received two bullets in his seat. As I proceeded with the dressing on the latter, I laughed a bit and told him, "This will mean a lot of lying on the stomach during the next two months."

He replied, "Yeh, but at least I'll be lying. I don't have to tell you what you'll be doing."

"Don't laugh too soon," I warned him. "You'll be back in a couple of months, and there'll still be lots of Germans to keep you from having your way."

I went over to the dead soldier and covered his face. "Another telegram and another Purple Heart," I muttered to myself.

When a captured enemy was searched, there were two prized trophies that the fellows looked for—watches and pistols. Most of the watches were very handsome looking and highly engraved. I found, however, that only one out of twenty was really a good watch. They had heavy gold or silver cases, and fine jeweled movements and had probably been handed down from father to son for several generations. The balance of the watches had very few jewels and gold-colored hands and cases. The one that I saw the most of was of French make. Perhaps the German army had contracted with some French factory, during the occupation years, to have it made at a special price. It was a handsome, standard-size pocket watch with an engraved silver or white metal back. The sides of the case were rose gold colored; before they were used long, however, the color wore off and exposed a white metal. It contained ten jewels, or rubies as they were called, in a cylinder movement. The balance wheel was in the center of the watch. By pushing a pin, located on the side of the case, with the thumbnail of one hand, and turning the stem with the other hand, the hands were moved for setting.

An infantryman gave me one of the better watches.

It was in a handsomely engraved silver case. On the back of the case were the words: "Otto Rose—Uhrmachermeister." When I opened the back of it, the red and amber jewels stared out at me. My, how large they were! They appeared approximately an eighth of an inch in diameter.

German wrist watches were not too plentiful, but occasionally I saw one that someone had taken from some high officer or aviator. It had a flashy expansion bracelet that most of the infantrymen did not care to wear. Shining jewelry of all types was strictly taboo with the infantry for they did not want their position betrayed by a reflection.

Pistols were good souvenirs and were practical. When a rifleman had to stand guard on a very dark, rainy night, it was much better to have a pistol in his pocket, poised with a finger on the trigger, than to have a rifle standing at his side. The enemy would have had to bump into him before he knew that anyone was around on these dark nights. Before he could get his rifle up the enemy could have taken advantage of the situation.

Then again pistols had their disadvantages. It was a standing rule never to be captured with souvenirs on one's person. Once we found ourselves thrown back several hundred yards and several of the fellows were captured. When we retook the ground we found that one of the fellows had been captured carrying an enemy pistol. They had shot him in the forehead with it. He was on his back with his shirt torn open, exposing a large X slashed across his chest. The pistol was lying upon it.

IV.

DURING the next few days the stiffening resistance of the enemy slowed us down considerably. We were entering the rich industrial region near the German border. The terrain was more difficult; there were more forests, hills, and industrial towns. The towns were made of brick, cement, and tile, and were much easier to defend than the mud walls and thatched roofs of Normandy. Here the people did not greet us with open arms as they had a couple of weeks before. They were more cautious, for they had seen us thrown back a few times. They had also seen what happened to the Frenchmen who greeted us after they had been pointed out by the German collaborationists.

Sometimes in mid-afternoon we entered a town in anticipation of taking it in a few hours. After a hard fight nightfall found us about halfway through it. The shouts of the cheering civilians gave us a good conception of the situation. Behind us we heard the rousing cry of *"Vive L'Amerique!"* while from the enemy territory we heard *"Vive L'Allemagne!"*

Several times, while entering a village, I listened to the same *"Vive L'Amerique,"* only to hear the haunting *"Vive L'Allemagne"* resounding with the echoes of our

54

retreating footsteps as we were being pushed back again.

The war was going from bad to worse, and the situation was becoming more desperate. No one could be trusted, for one could no longer tell a patriot from a spy. The local Frenchmen would not talk for one side or the other for fear of reprisal. They were afraid that perhaps the allies would lose the war.

To make the picture even darker, the enemy no longer respected the red cross of the non-combatant personnel. I heard several reports of their being killed or wounded—deliberately fired upon. Our lieutenant told me to be cautious, for the same thing could happen in this sector. I told him I'd be careful, but I gave it very little thought. Me being fired upon? Impossible. I had walked all over no man's land many times, and no one even pointed a weapon at me.

While waiting for the artillery to work over a small town before we entered it, we sat at the side of an asphalt road. It had been a hard, hot day, and we felt very tired. Perhaps that was why we did not take all the precautions we should have. We sat on the shoulder rather than in the ditch. It was a good deep ditch affording excellent protection, but perhaps the past few weeks had been too easy for us. Maybe we were growing soft or thought that the enemy was nowhere around.

Three of us, sitting close together, were engaged in a little conversation. A fellow named Terry sat between a machine gunner and myself. The conversation wandered from local events to England, to home, and then to our families.

Terry told us about his mother and fiance getting

along so well. We both agreed that it was wonderful, almost amazing. Usually they are a bit jealous of one another.

Suddenly the machine gunner plunged head first into the ditch. It looked like a very awkward feat, but both Terry and I thought little of it.

"He's a bit shaky. Maybe he thought he heard something," said Terry.

I skipped over the subject and got back to our former conversation.

"Had a letter lately from your fiance?" I asked, still staring at the machine gunner who lay in the ditch.

He did not answer, so I turned to see what had his attention. My glance was met by a horror-stricken stare. His eyes were bulging, his nostrils were large, and his mouth was opened very wide. His tongue stuck out as if he were being choked to death. He did not breathe. Then the blood came gushing up from his throat. As the blood reached the end of his tongue, a certain realization came to me. He had been shot in the neck.

The instinct for self-preservation seized me, and I gave Terry a jolting push on the shoulderblade. He toppled head first into the ditch. I dived for it at the same instant.

I saw the other men crawl back up the side of the ditch. Cautiously, they peered out and pointed their weapons across the road.

I looked at Terry. He quivered, then stiffened. He was dead. He would have been twenty-one in another month—just a boy who looked forward to manhood with great anticipation. I recalled that only yesterday he had asked if I thought he would reach the age of twenty-one. I couldn't tell him that. I knew that the average infantryman did not last that long. I pacified him by telling him that right then he was more of a man than seventy-five per cent of the males who had reached twenty-one. He liked that.

Even as I looked at Terry his clear blue eyes became cloudy. I straightened out his limbs and covered his face.

I crawled over to the machine gunner who was first to dive into the ditch. His head rested face downward in a pool of blood that was soaking into the dusty leaves and dead grass that cluttered the ditch. I saw that he had been hit in the back of the head with a bullet. I realized that he did not dive into the ditch, as Terry and I had thought, but was knocked in by the force of the bullet entering his head—killed without a sound.

A well-camouflaged sniper with telescopic sights on his rifle had been firing on us from a great distance. He was accurate but noiseless to us.

We were ordered to move out. In single file, we went up the ditch until we came to a small grove of trees. There, safe from the eyes of the sniper, we got back on the road again and headed for the next town.

Soon eighty-eight-millimeter shells began to rain down with little or no warning. All of them hit the road, and the explosions seemed to walk right up the asphalt at ten-yard intervals. The enemy artillerymen had done the same thing they did in Normandy; they knew all the distances right to the foot. With these exact measurements they could place a shell in the precise spot they wanted it.

We had to leave the road, for before long the shells would be falling where we were. Into the field we dashed.

With the perspiration running from us we headed single file for the little town. Suddenly the shells began to bear down upon us. We had outwitted the enemy, but not for long. His forward observer could see us, for once again those eighty-eights were dropping right where he wanted them.

We scattered and ran in various directions. No one went backward, but everyone headed in a general forward direction. Some jumped into holes recently dug by the enemy who had stayed here during the last day or so. I continued to run toward a fence about a hundred yards distant. As I passed one of the holes one of the fellows was climbing out, cussing very loudly.

"What's the matter, Joe? Are you hurt?" I asked.

"Hurt, hell! That's an old German straddle trench, and right now I don't smell like roses!"

Evening found us holding the line in a small pasture. A trench that had been dug and used in 1918 zigzagged across it.

As I sat in my foxhole and looked out across the field, I remembered the books and movies about the last war. So this was one of those trenches that used to be filled with mud and soldiers. Of course, that was twenty-six years ago, but I could imagine that they were just as young and afraid as we were. Perhaps my own father had been in this very spot at that time.

Some of the large trees near-by still bore the scars of World War I that hadn't healed in twenty-six years.

Any living thing that had been so deeply wounded would have a great tale to tell.

I looked at the nice green grass about me. Twenty-six years ago it had been oozing mud and flying clods. Two minutes from now it could again.

During the course of the few days past a large number of enemy troops had been surrounded. We were on the forward position of the northern flank of this pocket.

As our troops pressed them closer together the fighting became very intense. The enemy had become well organized and was determined to fight on. At first they were gathered a good distance from us, and we merely chased a few stragglers back to the larger group, but now they had organized and were striving to drive their way out of the pocket. Of course we stood between them and their freedom.

They must have had contact with the outside army, for several of their attacks had been co-ordinated. At times it seemed as if we were to be crushed between those two armies. It sounded as if the devil himself was having a nightmare and was on the rampage. Shells rained down and screamed and whistled over us from both directions. Sometimes I wondered if our own artillery could be mixed up and was firing upon us, but from all indications these were all enemy shells.

Dawn found us taking a terrific pounding with artillery. Soon it stopped, and we expected an attack from a wave of infantry.

Suddenly a thundering roar came to my ears. At first I was frightened, thinking that it was one of those secret weapons everyone had been talking about. As I looked out over the vast field to our left, I saw a huge cloud of black smoke. I looked more closely and saw it was a train coming down a railroad track that passed about a hundred yards in front of us. My God! It was impossible! A train roaring through no man's land. Perhaps they didn't know that we were this far inland. They must. We couldn't have been pounded so hard if they did not know that we were there.

As the train roared down upon us we learned that it was a relief train of troops and supplies to reinforce the surrounded enemy troops. What a way to do it!

Every man that we had, and every weapon that could be fired, was trained upon the track before us to await the train. A message was sent out by radio, explaining the unusual situation to the rest of the outfit down the line.

As it came into range the firing began. Everything was aimed at the locomotive, for it and it alone controlled the success or failure of their bold attempt. As the bullets hit the boiler, the steam began to spurt. The machine gunners did very well. Apparently most of the bullets were penetrating.

Suddenly there was a deafening explosion, a whistling scream, and another resounding blast. After a two or three second lull, there was a terrific roar which made the whole earth tremble. An anti-tank gun, set up behind us, had fired, making a direct hit. The locomotive blew up and now seemed dissolved in a huge cloud of steam.

The machine guns were raking the halted boxcars as German soldiers gushed forth from the open doors.

They crawled and ran and scattered, trying to flee in all directions. Some ran toward us with upraised hands in a dire attempt to surrender. Others tried to run away or dash for cover. One brave group attempted to set up a machine gun but were cut down before they could get it assembled. Our machine gunners were having a field day. They got all but a handful of those who jumped off the train on this side and a great portion of those who got off on the other.

Before long there were no more of the enemy to be fired upon, so all firing ceased. A white piece of cloth on a stick seemed to rise up out of the smouldering ground, and a soldier holding it rose slowly beneath it. I gritted my teeth and prayed that some trigger-happy member of the outfit wouldn't shoot him down. I knew that the older members knew better. They knew that it was much better to take prisoners than to fight it out. If that brave soldier was fired upon we would have to kill or capture every one of them. If they must be killed they certainly wouldn't stand and be slaughtered but would fight to the very end.

Our lieutenant stood up in his hole and motioned the surrendering soldier forward. I could see a wry smile come over that anxious enemy face. He motioned to others, who sprang up all about him. They marched toward us with their clasped hands resting upon their heads. The last two were carrying a wounded companion.

Each of them was thoroughly searched for weapons. At the same time they were relieved of any watches or valuable jewelry. I searched the wounded man and bandaged his wound with his aid packet. Then the entire group, thirty-eight in all, was taken to the rear with two of our men as guards.

The train was examined to make sure that no more enemy soldiers were about. I went to the locomotive and looked it over. There was a large hole in the earth beneath it, and the tracks were no longer there. A short time before it had been puffing and hissing, a breathing, belching monster, pulling its huge load leisurely over the moors. Now it rested powerless and helpless. The huge boiler was shattered into hundreds of ribbon-like strips. From a distance it looked like a huge shaving brush.

We approached a looming slag pile. Since it was late afternoon the lieutenant wanted to get past it by nightfall. It was much better to have it behind us overnight. Under the cover of darkness the enemy could become well entrenched and concealed in and about it. We well remembered the beating we took the time we failed to get past a huge gravel pile. That was long ago, in Normandy, but one lesson like that was enough to make us remember it a lifetime. The enemy had buried all types of weapons in the side of the mountain of gravel. With the aid of wooden boxes and tarpaulins they had concealed themselves as well as their weapons so that only the muzzles protruded. Dawn found them looking down upon us. Not being able to escape their view, we were forced to withdraw under a withering fire that cost us many good men.

Here the enemy was on three sides of us. We had advanced more rapidly than the outfits to our right and left.

As we moved toward the slag pile, I saw that it was still smouldering. The mine must have been in operation only a few hours ago. The soldiers approached it in a long single file. I brought up the rear.

By the time I reached the base of the dark pile, the first scout was well on his way around it. We all hoped that he would not find the enemy waiting on the other side.

All at once the cool stillness was broken by a barrage of incoming shells. The enemy, watching us for some time, had chosen this deadly moment to lash out. They had caught us unaware. The shells came from our right flank, a position that our own troops ordinarily occupied. This was different. Each day we learned something new. Just when we thought that we had undergone every experience possible, something new and different happened.

Six shells zoomed in. Five of the six hit the slag pile at the same instant, loosing a huge avalanche. I froze in my tracks, unable to move or speak. I knew that the rolling mass of heavy stone would miss me, but many of those before me were to be buried alive. Some looked up at it, and their faces turned into masks of horror as they leaped away, only to be quickly overtaken, crushed down, and buried under tons and tons of slag. Others did not even notice the avalanche crashing down upon them. I saw our lieutenant buried in his tracks while still walking on toward the enemy.

Those who were spared scurried away. I ran with them. At a safe distance we huddled together and peered back upon the smouldering blood-thirsty monster that had just claimed forty-two from our ranks.

63

The hot slag was still rolling, tumbling, and sliding down.

We would attack no more that day, for the fighting strength had been drained from our outfit. We had to burrow in and try to hold what we had gained. Our foxholes were dug deep and were stretched over a great distance for the number of men we had—only one man in a hole instead of the usual two.

Another unfortunate, unforgettable day drew to a close. As the evening dusk settled, the sun reflected a bright red, a bloody red, from the mountain of slag that loomed up so monstrously before us.

My eyes were filled with tears. This mass killing had stunned me for awhile. Perhaps I had taken it so long that I was at the breaking point. I needed a rest.

The sun had dropped behind us. It was dark, ever so dark, and the huge mountain before me was silhouetted by the flashes of the huge guns in the distance. Throughout the night it continued to blink on and off before me as if a screen in a theatre. It kept me reminded that it held the bodies and souls of forty-two of the finest and bravest men who had ever walked over this area. They had not had time to flee nor a chance to fight back. They had been caught from the back and side unaware, smashed down in a strictly one-sided fight.

Again the distant gun flashed. Again the grinning silhouette of the beastly slag pile. At times I thought I saw American soldiers at its base or on its side, but at the next flash they were gone.

The rising sun found us in the same position as on the night before. No one talked, but everyone was deep in thought. We hoped that replacements would filter in before we must plunge ahead or be attacked.

The artillery was booming, but it was landing a great distance away. Fighting clamored on both sides of us. Perhaps we would wait until the troops on each side came up in line with us. In the meantime we stole a little solitude of our own.

I plucked a poppy beside my foxhole and examined it carefully from end to end. The bright red petals and black seeds. The green leaves. I dissected them carefully and examined their fibers closely. I used to do this with plants and small animals in a biology class. There I had had to draw pictures of each part and remember its name. Here I examined it as carefully and recalled what I still remembered of it. My chain of thought was not so well linked here as it was back in the biology class. There I had had no interruptions and not a real worry in the world. The cross-currents of the past and future, both sparking with death, created a short circuit in my brain. Some high-powered transmitter crashed in on my frequency.

During the day the booming of the battle on each side drew close. Replacements came in. There were only twenty-four of them, but with them came the promise of more the following day.

By the time they all dug in, the line of battle on each side was even with us, so we ventured out again. By the expression on the faces of the new men I could see that they were uneasy. This was the smallest company they had ever been in. They knew from what they had been taught that a company required every man to show his best fighting.

As we moved away from the slag pile I glanced back at it. Within its massive bosom it possessed the bodies of my forty-two comrades. Would those fellows ever be found? Would anyone ever know what happened or know that they were there? Would they be removed, or would they be left under the debris? Perhaps they would always be on the list of the missing in action.

It was early fall but still not well enough along to bring coolness to the hot days. The nights, however, were becoming chillier. The dew on the grass and trees sparkled brightly each morning, and my clothing became very damp during the night. The moisture dripped from my helmet. Often it took until noon for my clothing to become thoroughly dry.

The small towns and villages straggled into one another here. By the time the last soldier had cleared a town the first man was preparing to enter another. Most of them had stone walls enclosing the inner portion beyond which the old towns had outgrown. Some of these walls and the older buildings still showed the patchwork put in after the damage of the last war. It had been raining very frequently lately, but even during the hot dry days the damp, dark walls were wet and shiny. They even smelled foul.

A young replacement was always wandering around looking for souvenirs. Often I had to search for him when the outfit moved out again. Perhaps he was too young and foolish to realize the danger of walking around alone. Maybe he did not have the experience or comprehension he should. Often when looking for him I prayed that he had not been harmed. He was young

66

and completely ignorant of the dangers about him. He did not yet have a beard.

I felt responsible for the well-being of every man in the organization, and especially for the replacements. I tried to watch over them and teach them all I could from my experience until they had had the first scrap with the enemy.

This young fellow kept me busy at all times. Twice I had had to yell at him to duck down when we were fired upon. He always seemed to be looking far away—never watching what he was doing. His uniform hung on him like a sack. He hadn't developed enough to fill it properly—a poor-looking soldier. Adams was a poor soldier, but so terribly lucky that he came out unharmed from a situation, where by all the rules, he should have been killed or wounded. Perhaps someone besides myself was looking over him.

We came upon a large wooded area split by an open, barren field about two hundred yards square. The enemy was near-by in force. Our company divided and went through the woods on each side. I chose the group with our new lieutenant.

About halfway up the side of the field we came upon the enemy. I lay behind a large tree at the edge of the field while the bullets buzzed, whined, and splattered as they sought their way through the trees.

Suddenly a soldier from the woods on the other side of the field came dashing toward us. It was young Adams. The dirt flew all about his feet as the enemy machine guns tried to get him. He made the woods, hit the ground, and crawled to the lieutenant. After obtaining a radio battery he made the same gallant dash back across the open field. How he made it was beyond my imagination. Perhaps he had a charmed life.

After the enemy was subdued and the company was once again brought together I bandaged the wounds of two walking wounded and sent them back to the aid station. Everyone was accounted for but Adams.

"Maybe he got cut down on the way back across the field," suggested the lieutenant.

"I saw him make it okay," I told him. "By the way, what did he want the battery for?"

"Probably for the radio. The old battery must have been too weak."

"But the radioman was with us."

The lieutenant looked about in disgust, then told the company to lie low, keep a sharp lookout, and wait for him. He took me and another soldier to look for Adams.

A short way back we came upon an old house. Looking in the window, we saw Adams sitting in the middle of the floor, watching a toy train go around a small track. That was why he wanted the battery! He had risked his life, as well as ours, to pull a foolish trick.

The tongue lashing that the lieutenant gave him was one that should last for a long time. From the glare in the lieutenant's eyes I sometimes thought that he might shoot him to save his breath.

It was the last of September. A cold constant rain that soaked completely through and chilled to the marrow was coming more frequently, almost every night. My nose ran constantly, yet I did not appear to have a cold. Everyone was thoroughly dampened, whether he had a raincoat or not. About half the company had raincoats. If one didn't wear one the rain soaked through to the skin. Those who wore them were saturated by the moisture given off by the body. Many of the soldiers did not realize this, and they claimed that the coat leaked, that it strained the rain.

News came that some American troops had entered Germany from Belgium. It aroused some talk, but most of us thought that they would be stopped soon. The lines of supply were getting too long. Of course we would have liked to see them spearhead a drive into the country and end the whole thing, but it didn't seem logical. The least that most of us hoped was that it might relieve the pressure that had been stiffening in our area during the last few weeks.

We came upon a swollen, muddy river with many small concrete pillboxes on the opposite side. At first it looked as if we were in for a terrible fight, looking down the muzzles of those protruding arms. It seemed as if here we were to be stopped and slaughtered.

A night patrol proved to us that it wouldn't be as bad as it looked. The pillboxes were flooded by the muddy waters of the onrushing river and were not being operated very efficiently. Some were not occupied at all.

During the predawn hours of rainy blackness, artillery from both sides had it out. Our artillery had been brought up directly behind us, and then machine guns were entrenched along the river bank. They were to fire a protecting cover of bullets over the heads of the riflemen who would soon come and attempt to cross in rubber boats.

Before long they came—the dirty, unshaven, drenched

riflemen. They did not talk, but just went about their task of getting prepared to cross the cold, black waters of some unheard-of river. They slipped and slid in the slippery mud that lined the river bank and bottom. Large gobs of it stuck to their shoes, giving their feet a monstrous appearance. I saw all of this in the light-ninglike flashes from the artillery batteries which were booming and thundering all about us. The shadows leaped and dashed like some devil spirit in a hideous death dance.

I became a little nervous, so I tried curling my toes and then stretching them out again. It was not very difficult, for my feet fit loosely in my shoes; they were shriveled and shrunken from having been soaked in the cold, dirty water for several hours. There was very little feeling in them. I tried working them faster, thinking it might stimulate them and make them warm, but it did not. Before long they became too tired and I ended the squishing noise.

A number of the riflemen climbed into the rubber boats. Their bewhiskered faces were grim and taut, but still they said nothing.

All at once their officer gave the signal, and they shoved off. Hardly had they started when the enemy opened up on them. Our machine guns answered back. The blackness of the rainfilled night was filled with arches of tracer bullets. Between each pair of tracers were four steel bullets that were unseen dealers of death.

The enemy bullets began to splatter in the soft mud near us. Some of the tracers still sizzled red, and smoked in the mud, while others hit the water before us and glanced up and over. We were not very far from the enemy guns.

I saw men diving, falling, and jumping out of the rubber boats. The surging waters quickly devoured them and carried them swiftly away. I watched another boat shove off before me. The men squatted and cowered in it. One man in the rear knelt and paddled very rapidly. He was hit and toppled out. Another seized the paddle and took his place. He paddled feverishly before he was hit. Another replaced him. The boat continued on its way until in midstream it halted and began to drift. All that were aboard had been knocked out of action. Quickly it was carried away, taking its cargo of dead and dying with it. Others did the same thing. I watched them disappear in the ribbons of death made by the gun flashes on the water.

I felt helpless, for many could be saved if they received aid. It ate my heart away to witness this. These young boys, who looked so aged, were American. They were taking this as only Americans do. I had watched many nationalities undergo this strain, but only the Americans fought anything, anywhere, without question or hesitation, and bled without a sound. The youngest died with only a whimper. It gnawed at my very soul.

As I watched the powerless boats drift downstream I wondered what would become of the occupants. Only a few hundred yards down the river the enemy was in possession of both sides. Perhaps they would help them. Maybe they would think differently when they saw boatloads of men wearing American weapons and helmets approaching. It might appear to them as some fiendish attack and they would machine-gun the little remaining life out of the riddled rubber boats.

By ten o'clock some of the pillboxes directly across from us had been silenced. Our infantrymen occupied them. The rubber boats were reaching the other bank in greater numbers, but some still floated helplessly downstream.

After some time it was our turn. The rain still came down, driven by a steady wind. I crawled from my water-filled hole toward the near-by loaded boat. When I slid down the slippery bank of the river and into the muddy water, it washed off most of the heavy mud that clung to my shoes. I climbed aboard and we shoved off. The bullets began to buzz and whine; they splashed into the water all about us. One ripped into the large rubber roll that formed the side of the boat. Everyone crouched low.

As we hit the bank on the other side everyone jumped out of the boat and dived into the mud and tall grass. The river bank was not so high over here, and there were two or three inches of water on the ground.

We inched our way up to a concrete pillbox with about a foot of water in it and crawled in.

The fighting continued, the machine guns clattered, and the riflemen moved ahead. Soon the mortar shells began to land all about, making the fight hard and long for each contested inch of water-soaked earth we gained.

Now we moved up again. As I crawled through the deep grass I looked back and saw the engineers constructing a bridge across the river behind us. The mortar shells were raining about them.

There was a large city immediately in front of us. I had always wondered about the taking of a large city, but after learning the layout I shuddered. It was not just an ordinary city, but a huge fortress that had been impregnable for well over a century. It consisted of seventeen forts.

I learned that there were other divisions converging on it. Tanks, which must have come across the bridge that our engineers had built, were crawling up.

By midafternoon the rain ceased, but the sun did not shine. Just ahead lay a large brick building, a factory that made the red tile used on the roofs. The enemy had decided to use it as an outer defense for the fortress city.

At first our infantry attempted to take it, but were easily beaten back. From the amount of firepower they met, we knew that there were plenty of men, weapons, and ammunition in it.

Our artillery zeroed in on it, taking three shots to do this, the first hitting a privy and blasting it into oblivion, the second knocking a gaping hole in a large brick chimney, and the third hitting the factory itself, but doing little damage. Then several other guns got a line on it and began pumping shells into it.

Before long dive bombers appeared overhead and worked it over as the tempo of the artillery increased. Then dozens of tanks started their motors, creating a pall of blue-black smoke.

The planes ceased their bombing and hovered overhead. A short time later the artillery was silent and the tanks crawled forward with the infantry crouched low behind them as they fired their machine guns and cannons at the crumbling building.

As we got closer, I saw that the building was merely a smoking shell. The shooting of the enemy was wild but determined.

When close enough, some of the infantrymen yelled at the enemy to surrender. The shooting stopped, and they staggered out of the dust-filled, smoking ruins. They did not come directly toward us in an orderly fashion as they usually did, but staggered and stumbled with their hands over their heads, their eyes closed. Most of them were coughing, and their faces and clothing were covered with the bright red powder used in making the tile. One of the bombs had landed in the factory's stock pile.

They were searched before I assembled them in a small group and made them sit down. They continued to cough. I looked at their eyes, but there was little I could do. I soaked gauze with water and washed their eyes out, but still none of them could see. Perhaps they never would.

Before they could be sent back we had to capture someone who could see to lead them. We could afford but one man to guard them on the way back; consequently, he must stay behind them at all times.

As we waited one of them mumbled a bit how disgusting it was to fight so hard with so little and still lose. Surrendering was the only thing left after they had been hit so hard first by the airplanes, then by the artillery, and finally by the tanks and infantry. No one could hold out against that.

I asked him if he minded being blinded. With his eyes

closed and the tears streaming down his cheeks he looked up at me and said in broken English, "It is just one of the misfortunes of war."

Another prisoner came running toward us with upraised hands. One of the riflemen had sent him because he had been unharmed.

I got the prisoners up and into line. Each put his right hand upon the shoulder of the prisoner ahead of him with the unharmed prisoner at the head. A rifleman was sent to guard them on their way toward the rear. As they started off I hurried to catch up with my company.

It began to rain again. We fought in rain or in sunshine—mostly in rain. This game of war was different from any other game I had ever played. It was not like a baseball game, where foul weather might have postponed the game; nothing like a boxing bout where a foul may cause one to lose. He who played the roughest and dirtiest usually won.

We fought on in the cold drenching rain. It was much better to be defending a position than to be attacking it, for usually the defenders had a shelter not only from the weather but from the flying bullets and shrapnel. We had to run across open spaces, expose ourselves to the enemy gunsights and the driving rain— the cold, damnable rain. We slid in the sticky mud and crawled through the tall, wet grass, keeping us thoroughly saturated and flipping cold water into our faces and down our necks. It cut our hands and made them sting and ache. Our skins became shriveled and senseless; our whole bodies were numb.

I did not know the date of the month nor the day

of the week; it did not matter. However, I knew the sound of an incoming shell, and my ears and mind automatically recorded the distance from me that it would land. If it were close, my legs instinctively buckled, and I fell to the ground; I closed my eyes, my mouth opened wide. I knew automatically that my mouth must be open or the blast would shatter my eardrums. When all these terrible noises of battle came to my ears it was a steady clamor. Often when someone talked to me, he had to come right up beside my ear or I could not hear him. My ears seemed to have shut out all smaller noises.

The fighting carried on from house to house, from yard to yard. Often I saw a head appear and a face peek cautiously from within some upstairs window expecting to look across the street and see some enemy face or weapon peering from another house window. Someone across the street would do the same. Then, suddenly, both would rise with a smile and one less crisis to cope with.

I crawled cautiously beside the long, low back stone fence of several lots in a block. Each lot was separated by a similar stone fence. The houses were at the other end of the lots, facing the other way. As I crawled along, I rose to my knees and looked over the fence into each yard to make sure there were no enemy soldiers there—that I had not gone too far.

In the middle of the block I saw an American rifleman crawling from yard to yard across each partitioning fence. I crouched down again and crawled on to the next yard. There I saw an enemy soldier headed in the opposite direction. He would reach this partitioning fence in the same place and about the same time as this American rifleman.

I wished to cry out and warn my brother in arms, but I could not. I knelt there in the wet grass with my mouth gaping in astonishment—a ringside seat for the performance.

They reached the small stone fence at the same time. The caution they used made me think that they each suspected something unfriendly on the other side, for each got to his knees, brought his rifle barrel up even with his line of sight, and gradually, cautiously, rose to have a look at the other side.

The American came up a bit more rapidly, a decisive move that determined the winner. As the American's eyes came up to the top of the fence, the enemy helmet had just appeared and he quickly adjusted his rifle. It faced the helmet squarely in the center and as the helmet cleared the top and the eyes appeared he pulled the trigger. The enemy went over backwards. He did not topple, but leaped as if in a back dive from a springboard, and landed a full six feet from the fence.

I looked back at the American. He was on his hands and knees hugging the fence. He was about to pull the pin from a grenade and toss it over to take care of anything in the next yard.

I yelled at him, "Hey, Joe! Hold it! No one else over there."

He looked up in astonishment, then smiled. Quickly, he jumped the fence and was beside me.

"Whew! That was close," he gasped.

"You can consider yourself plenty lucky. You kept your head though when you saw that guy, and that probably saved you. It's a good thing you didn't get excited and pull a boner."

"Didn't get excited? Huh! If you'd say 'boo' right now, I'd fill my britches."

We rested for a few seconds. Two shells screamed in.

"Let's go," he said.

"I can't go with you. I've got to stay alone, or I'll get bumped off. The only person I can be seen with is someone who has been knocked out of action."

"You're right."

He crawled off.

The roar of the tanks, the screaming of shells, and the rattle of machine guns grew louder. The struggle seemed to be coming to a climax. It could not stay so fierce and heated very long; something had to give.

I crawled up the gutter of a cobblestone street. The rain made the street glare; water ran down the gutter. I lay down in it, for it was the lowest place that I could find. As I felt the water run through my clothing and past my skin, I wished that I could go with it down the street, down the gutter, or down the drain—anywhere but in this street.

Our tanks were everywhere, shooting at everything, but still everything shot back. They machine-gunned the houses, setting some on fire, and blasted big holes in every building.

Once again I heard that old familiar double explosion connected by a whistling scream. It was an enemy tank which had made an appearance about two blocks up the street. Apparently the tank beside me had not seen it, for it continued to machine-gun the buildings. There was no way that I could warn them for they were buttoned up and the roar of the battle was too loud. I could picture just what would happen; I had seen it before. The enemy tank would send a shell ripping into it; and no one inside would ever know what had hit them.

They sent another shell. It hit the building beside me with a glancing blow, knocking large pieces of rock and mortar down upon me, clanking upon my helmet. I was thankful that it was an armor-piercing shell—a type which did not explode.

The main objection to being fired upon by a tank or a self-propelled gun was that it did not give any warning, for the range was too close. The first sound was the impact when it hit, then the whistle of its flight, and finally the explosion when it was fired. It seemed somewhat like running a motion picture or a record backward.

A fear of being hit by flying pieces of the tank seized me. If it were hit on this side, I would most certainly be injured.

I began to inch myself backward down the gutter through the filthy water. I could not get up and run, for there was no room between bullets for a human being. I watched the enemy tank for a flash from his gun, for it may give me warning enough to drop my head before the shell hit. It wasn't much, but I figured it might make the difference between life and death. As I watched I saw sparks flying from the stone streets where the rifle and machine gun bullets hit.

Then I saw it—a flash and a puff of smoke. It didn't look like the real thing, so I did not duck. The enemy tank seemed to have turned a bit so that it did not face us squarely. It had been hit by someone or something from a side street.

There was a terrific explosion beside me. It deafened me for a moment. I felt as though I had been picked up and thrown down again into the gutter. The skin on my face felt tight, and my eyebrows and eyelashes seemed to have disappeared. The tank beside me had fired a round into the already crippled enemy tank and the muzzle flash had seared my face and filled my lungs with the smell of sulphur.

I looked at the enemy tank. Black smoke billowed from the enemy tank as a wounded man crawled from its hatch. He was instantly hit with a dozen bullets. He reared over backward and hung from the hatch by his knees, his arms dangling and his unbuttoned tunic hanging down over his face.

And so it went from house to house, street to street, and gutter to gutter.

As I went into the basement of one of the large buildings a middle-aged man with a mustache stumbled past me, then fell to the floor clasping his head. He seemed half dazed. I knelt beside him and pulled his hand away, but he fought to keep it there. A woman knelt on the other side and volunteered to help, so I had her hold his hand.

The right portion of his forehead had been blown off, exposing his brain. There was little I could do, so I put an amount of sterile absorbent cotton on it, then bandaged it. I was careful not to bandage it too tightly.

I motioned to the woman that we were finished. She jumped up and motioned for me to follow her into another room. On a bed lay a young girl about sixteen years old. Her hair was heavy and dark, her skin, a chalky white. She appeared unconscious or in a deep sleep, and her breathing was almost unnoticeable. She was truly a picture of young beauty.

The woman pulled the sheet down to the girl's waist, exposing her naked body. On her right side, just to the right of her firm white breast, was a gaping, scarlet hole. I placed my hand on her forehead; it was warm. I held her wrist and took a quick feel of her pulse; it was fast and faint.

I got on my knees beside the bed to get a better look at the wound, while the woman held a lighted candle for me to see. It was the familiar type of a puncture wound; she must have had a piece of shrapnel buried in her chest or lung. The wound did not bleed, but there was a slight, watery discharge. She should have been sent to surgery.

There was little I could do but tell the woman to take her to a hospital as soon as she could—if she ever got a chance or if a hospital were left.

I sprinkled sulfa powder on the wound, applied a small dressing, and taped it in place. I rose and began to walk away, but the woman grabbed my arm again. She had pulled the sheet the rest of the way down and now pointed to another similar wound in the girl's groin. This wound was not bleeding either, but apparently it had ruptured some blood vessels, for the flesh about the wound was colored a dark blue.

I placed my hand on the girl's soft, white abdomen. It felt like plush velvet, but it was warm. I was not sure, but I thought it should have been cool.

Again I used the sulfa powder, the dressing, and the adhesive tape. After putting the sheet back up around her neck, I turned to the woman, and with the best signs and language that I could think of, I told her to get the girl to a hospital as soon as possible. She seemed to understand. She shook my hand with both of hers and kissed it.

Outside the battle still raged with all its fury. Our casualties seemed light, and very few were wounded badly. Plenty of men, machinery, and firepower helped us greatly, especially in giving us confidence.

We came to a large, open area, apparently used for a play ground or a drill field. At one end was an innocent-looking building which someone had already discovered to be a pillbox in disguise.

Three tanks converged on it. When about a hundred yards from it, the two tanks on the outside stopped and leveled their cannons. The center tank, a tankdozer, continued up to the very door of the pillbox, scooped a huge mound of earth against the door, then backed up to its two companions. Together they began firing seventy-five and seventy-six millimeter shells at it. I could see some that glanced off, but most of them carved quite a nick into the pillbox.

Very soon a white flag began to fly. The firing ceased, and the tankdozer proceeded to remove the earth from the door. Nine prisoners walked out with their hands high over their heads. This was another bit of American ingenuity—using brains rather than brawn.

Several companies now attempted to force the surrender of one of the huge forts. Many tanks rolled up against it and huge artillery batteries, from far in the rear, heaped monstrous shells upon it mercilessly, while our mortars silenced the antiaircraft battery which was embedded on the top of this large mountain of concrete. This forced the fort to be closed very tightly, giving the infantry a chance to place large satchel and pole charges against the huge steel doors. Some of them contained as much as a thousand pounds of TNT.

A few explosions from those charges soon blasted the doors open, exposing a long concrete corridor. Along the walls were steel doors which led into the many compartments of the fort.

A short gun battle ensued in the corridor, and once again satchel charges were used on the steel doors. After each door was blown open, a hot fight progressed.

Before many of the doors were blown open, the rest opened voluntarily. Rifles barked and machine guns began to purr. Bullets glanced from wall to wall along the corridor, and men were falling fast. Soon our men were forced to withdraw.

A tank pulled up to the door and leveled its large gun to fire several rounds into the corridor. Each shot moved the tank to one side or the other. Sometimes it fired so fast that the gunner did not have time to adjust the aim between shots. I could hear the projectile strike the sides of the corridor two or three times before hitting the end. It did not explode, but must have hit sidewise and did not set off the fuse on the tip. Sometimes I could hear them roll around a bit before they came to a final halt. Those that exploded created a roaring thunder that echoed and shook the entire countryside.

Once again the infantry rushed in and a fight ensued.

I went in with them and carried out the wounded. It was hard to see and to breathe, for the place was full of smoke and fumes. It took many hours and many casualties to clear the entire fort.

I looked over the huge supplies of ammunition and food. If they had fought a bit harder, or had not been hit so hard, they could have held out rather comfortably for many months. We spent many casualties and fired a tremendous amount of ammunition to take it, but perhaps it was worth it. By-passing it we would have lived in constant fear of such a powerful monster lying behind our lines. In the end, it would have had to be taken anyway.

We were to hold up here for awhile to wait for more supplies. There was still a long way to go, and many more powerful forts had to be taken before we possessed the entire city.

I talked with some of the tank drivers. Most of them had a very short supply of fuel and could not acquire any more. They thought that perhaps the bridge on the river behind us had been knocked out, and that it should be repaired or replaced in a day or so, so that we would have plenty of gasoline to run the tanks. In the meantime we hoped the enemy would not counterattack.

I noticed that when our artillery observer called for artillery to be fired upon a target, the artillerymen asked if it were a positive target or just a possible one. If it were a possible one, they told him to make sure one way or another; they would fire on positive targets only.

Up to this time if there were any possible target in

the area they lost no time zeroing in on it. If the observer had requested five shells, he usually saw ten or a dozen come in. Now if he requested five, he felt lucky to see two or three.

I began to feel that there was something more than a bridge failure holding back supplies, for the artillery pieces were located on the other side of the river. I gave it a lot of thought, but said nothing. Perhaps the supply lines were getting too long; maybe the submarines were sinking the supply ships, or we may even have been surrounded some distance to the rear.

During our stay I made the most of the situation by setting up a little aid station of my own. Even though it was in the center of a battlefield, it was one of the safest, soundest places in the world, for this fort had foot upon foot of reinforced seasoned concrete on all sides. My greatest objection to this near perfect setup was my having to go out and gather up business. It turned out often to be as dangerous as it was laborious.

The electricity in the fort had been shut off, and the only source of light that I could find came from candles I had liberated from a near-by church. It took a lot of them, for I had to have one burning at all times to light the room. Requisitioning from a house of God made me feel a bit shameful, so I took only enough to last throughout each day.

Near the doorway of the room I had a litter resting upon two boxes. On a third box I had two candles set in empty cognac bottles. This was my operating table. I lit the candles only when there was a patient to bandage.

By arranging half a dozen litters on the floor side by

side, I made a good resting place for the wounded who were waiting for the litter bearers to come for them.

The bearers came whenever I called for them, but at this time they made only two trips every twenty-four hours—one just as soon as darkness came and another before the break of dawn. The street fighting was too hot and close for anyone to venture out into it unnecessarily.

Suddenly the lieutenant poked his head through the doorway of my concrete dressing station, "You've got one hour to clear out of here. Get the wounded evacuated and stick close to the company." He disappeared again into the exploding hell outside. I didn't even have time to answer.

I had six soldiers waiting for evacuation, and none of them were really walking cases. I thought hard for a long moment. There was but one way out of this situation.

Three of the fellows could make it if they were given a bit of mental conditioning, so I explained the difficult situation, gave them directions for the safest return, and then assured them that they could make it if they tried hard.

I dashed outside and began asking all the soldiers I came across if they had seen any German prisoners of war. The third one I asked pointed to a blasted building.

"We're collecting them in the basement over there," he snorted. "Haven't taken many lately. We're not fighting that kind of war right now."

The lieutenant was lying in a shellhole in some rubble a few feet away, so I crawled over and rolled in beside him. He was firing a carbine at a burning house in the next block.

"How's things, Doc?" he yelled.

"Need some help," I told him.

"Can I help any?"

"You sure can. Let me borrow your forty-five for the next hour."

"You nuts?" he exclaimed. "You'd get in trouble for having it, and I'd get in trouble for letting you take it."

I explained to him about the six fellows back in the fort. I told him that I needed six prisoners to act as litter bearers for the three who could not walk and that the pistol would be used to keep the prisoners under control.

His forty-five hung from his hip, but he reached inside his jacket and took a Luger from a shoulder holster. Placing it on a brick between us, he said, "There's a loaded pistol. Take it. I suggest that you keep it under cover, especially when you are in view of the enemy."

As I picked it up, he added, "Remember, I did not give it to you. You found it on the brick."

"I won't forget," I assured him.

I pulled the clip out of the pistol. It was full. I replaced it, racked the mechanism on top of the barrel that put the shell into the chamber, and fired it into the air. It worked fine. Then I jammed it into the belt at my stomach.

I ran to the building which held the prisoners and went down the outside stairway into the basement. One could easily see why they had picked this building for the purpose, for there was but one way out, and that was the stairway facing the American line. No one could come out without staring into the muzzles of at least four or five American rifles. They were so shorthanded that they could not spare a man for guard duty alone, so this was an ideal setup.

There were seven prisoners. I had to have an even number to have litter bearer teams, so I chose the six strongest-looking ones and prepared to leave. The seventh begged so hard to go along that I finally consented to allow him. I led the way up the stairs, so the American riflemen and machine gunners would not think they were trying to escape and shoot them down. Then I allowed them to precede me. With upraised hands they broke into a jolting trot; they were headed for the rear of the American lines and perhaps safety.

It was just a short distance to the fort, and, once inside, I hastily prepared the six wounded Americans for evacuation. The three litter cases were to be transported by six of the prisoners.

Of the three remaining cases, one had his head and eyes bandaged from a scalp and facial wound, one a leg wound, and the other a shoulder wound. I stood them all up. The one with the leg wound was supported between the other two. The fellow with the bandaged head asked me to be sure they went in the right direction, for he could not see and didn't wish to get lost at this time.

The soldier with the leg wound had each arm about the shoulders of his supporting comrades. Removing the Luger from my belt, I pressed it into his right hand, "Go out the door, turn left, and keep going on that street. Use this to keep the litter bearers in hand. It is cocked and loaded; just pull the trigger. For heaven's sake, don't use it unless you have to. Six lives depend on this flimsy setup, so be careful. If you get tired, pick a safe place and rest."

Tears came to my eyes as the remaining prisoner and I watched the weary group struggle off.

Soon a group of machine gunners came running past the fort. Half a block back they set up the machine gun in the middle of the street. They were retreating in an orderly fashion and would hold fire on the enemy so the others could retreat.

Before long others came and I decided that it was about time I should fall back a block or so. I took off on the run. The prisoner was at my heels with his hands raised high above his head.

Another American was severely wounded. Another litter case. After dressing his wound I fashioned a stretcher from two drapery poles, the prisoner's coat, and my field jacket. After fastening all buttons on both coats, I placed them on the ground, one just above the other, with the buttons up. I then slid one pole up into one coat and out through its left sleeve, then up into the other coat and out through its left sleeve. I did the same with the other side. The prisoner and I carried him off.

Realizing that I must stay with the company, I got the first able-bodied citizen I saw to take my place on the litter before I turned back toward the company— my battle-weary, bleeding company.

When I came within a half block of the machine gun that was set up in the middle of the street, the bullets became thick again. I had to get down and crawl, so

I stopped for a moment. The street ran slightly up-grade; I could just peer over the crest and see the tanks battling it out a few blocks ahead. If the enemy should get past our armor they would come gushing down the street.

The air was heavy and damp, and my shirt hung cold and wet on my shoulders. I shivered a bit and wished that I still had my jacket. Perhaps I could find another.

While crawling the rest of the way to the machine gun, I could see half a dozen of our tanks slugging it out at close range with the enemy—too close. Some were in bad positions.

I lay flat on the stone street beside the machine gunner. His teeth were bared and tight together; the gun shook his entire body as he fired a steady stream of steel at the enemy. An occasional drop of rain landed on the barrel and sizzled into steam in an instant.

I yelled at him, "What's wrong with those fellows? Why don't they do something about the jam they're in?"

Without taking his eyes from the target, he yelled back, "They're out of gasoline. They're trapped!"

I could see that one of the tanks had ceased firing; it was out of ammunition. Its occupants scrambled out and two of them dashed into a near-by building, while the other two were shot down in the street behind them. Their bodies shuddered and convulsed as large-caliber bullets were still pumped into their lifeless forms.

One by one the tanks were given up or knocked out of action, until there no longer remained a line of defense in front of us. The enemy began to close in.

Turning to the machine gunner, I sang out, "Let's get moving."

"Just a minute. I want to give this one joker a couple more squirts."

Suddenly he was hit in the right wrist; his hand flew off and landed in the street a few feet away. He gripped the squirting artery in his teeth and continued to fire at the onrushing enemy.

An enemy soldier fell a block up the street, then the machine gunner turned to me, "Okay, you can take me away, Doc."

Quickly I removed a shoestring from one of his shoes and tied it tightly about his forearm. Throwing him over my shoulder in the form of a fireman's carry, I took off on the run down the street.

As I looked back at the blazing hell behind I could see the ammunition bearer coming after me; he had the machine gun under his arm.

The burden of my wounded comrade became increasingly difficult. My temples throbbed; my eyes bulged; my mouth was open wide, gasping for air, and I felt my heart thundering within my chest. In a stooped position I continued to lumber on. My entire insides felt like jelly, bouncing with each quaking step. With my right arm and hand, I held his body about my neck and shoulders. I swung my left arm freely to maintain balance.

A sudden jerk on my left hand spun me half around, and I lost my balance. With a jolting thud I hit the street, face first. My helmet was all that kept my head from being crushed by the weight of the wounded soldier.

Rolling the soldier off my body, I looked at my outstretched left hand. A bullet had passed through the palm. I moved all the fingers; it had not severed any bones or tendons. For that I was grateful.

At this moment the ammunition bearer came stumbling past. His legs were wide apart and on the verge of buckling. Blood oozed from the corners of his mouth.

I looked at the soldier beside me. At first he seemed unconscious, but soon I could see that he was dead, not of a severed right hand, but of a bullet in the back. He had been hit as I carried him.

The sparks flew as the bullets glanced off the stone street. I could not afford time to cover the face of the dead, for by this time the ammunition bearer had fallen. I crawled to him. He lay curled up on his side, hugging the machine gun closely with both arms. It reminded me of a sleeping baby clutching its favorite rag doll. There was nothing I could do for him.

After getting well into the wooded area I stopped to catch my breath and to bandage my hand. I breathed through my mouth, for my nose was clogged with blood from being bumped when I had fallen in the street.

The roar of battle still pounded at my eardrums, and the enemy was close on the heels of the retreating Americans. One could see the expression of tiredness and fear written on each fleeing soldier's face. They possessed a stolid, blank-faced fear that was different from that they had experienced before.

When I located my outfit again, I found that there was not too much left of it. They were well organized and were now under the command of a Lieutenant Ulman. He was a second lieutenant fresh from West Point. I knew that he would not be with us long, for I had seen them before. They were smart, well trained, and had more courage than most soldiers. If their exceptional courage did not get them killed within the first few weeks, they were rapidly promoted and sent back to higher headquarters. For them, actual front line duty was short, whichever way they went. If I had been an infantryman, I would not have been afraid to follow one of them through hell and high water.

As I dug a hole for myself I watched Lieutenant Ulman go to the various machine gun positions. He looked clean and fresh; even his clothing was still neat and clean. His newly shaven face shone for it did not possess the deep, dark creases of the battle-weary. He seemed strong and agile as he crawled and walked, each movement deliberate and expressive. It would have been an inspiration to fight under a man like that. But I knew, we all knew, how he would look in a day or two.

When he came to me, he looked at the slow progress with which I was getting my hole dug.

"What's the matter, tired?" he asked.

I said nothing, just held up my poorly bandaged left hand.

"How did you get hurt?"

"Got hit coming out of that town," I told him.

"Let's see," he peeked under the bandage which was stuck to the palm as well as to the back of my hand. I drew it back a bit for it hurt.

He looked up with a wrinkled forehead. "You had better go back," he blurted.

"I'm afraid I'd never make it. It's almost dark, and I doubt if I could find the bridge across the river. I'll wait until tomorrow and see how things turn out."

"Okay, you're the doctor," he said, as he picked up my shovel to finish digging the hole.

The night was a restless one. The Germans shelled us continually. They were firing a little long, for the shells crashed just behind us. Their screaming kept us awake and on the alert. My hand throbbed a continual message of pain. It had swollen, for I could feel that the bandage was tight.

The rain fell intermittently, and I shivered beneath the blanket I had wrapped around my body. It had been given to me by Lieutenant Ulman because I had no jacket.

The gray of dawn found everyone awake and alert, waiting for the attack that, in all probability, would come gushing from the walls of the smouldering city before us that possessed so many American tanks and American bodies. We had been forced out of it because of the lack of artillery support and gasoline—a costly and tragic retreat.

Soon enemy soldiers came swarming forth. They were allowed to advance to about mid-distance, and were then pinned down by small-arms fire. The mortars worked them over until very few were left.

A lone tank ventured out. The call was sent back for artillery. The first shell went over it, but the second found its mark and scored a direct hit. The tank was put out of action and set on fire. Everyone looked about at each other and winked, as a sign of assurance.

94

An hour passed. We were shelled for a few minutes and then the enemy sent more soldiers to be slaughtered, so most of us thought. This time they were supported by two light tanks. The call was again sent back for more artillery.

A considerable amount of calculation went on before they agreed to fire the first round. It finally came in, but missed by a couple of yards. It was reported back, and another round was asked for. A slow, heart-sickening answer came through, "Sorry, we have used our quota for today." The information was passed among the men, and the order was given to fight it out. The attack was stopped—stopped dead by the sheer guts of the infantry.

As the day passed slowly by, we were forced back. Stronger and more determined attacks came, and we were pushed to within a hundred yards of the river bank. The concrete pill boxes were immediately behind us.

In the early afternoon mail arrived by the company runner. I received two letters. One was from Mother, the other from a soldier friend who was still stationed in the United States.

The letter from Mother tried to be cheerful, but I read between the lines. She was worrying constantly about my welfare. Her letter was not too cheerful and spicy; it was plain and blunt. She enclosed a few newspaper clippings. They were death notices of three of my closest friends. Each clipping had a picture of the fellow. They were all in the prime of health with broad smiles, and proudly displaying their uniforms. They had been killed in Normandy. I had grown up with them—knew their families, their hobbies, their likes and dislikes.

They had all been killed in France. That was why Mother sent the clippings—to emphasize the need for me to be careful. Yes, I would be careful, I promised myself. I would write and tell her that I would. It might ease her mind.

Being careful sometimes helped, but here life was more like a game of chance. It was not always how careful you were, but where you were when certain things happened. There were times when I had moved just seconds before the place that I had previously occupied was blown to bits. Other times I had stayed while others moved away only to be killed or mutilated by artillery fire. So in that respect there was no way of being careful. Of course, there were many precautions that one could take, but most of them were instinctive.

I would have written and explained these things to Mother, but she wouldn't have understood. No one would ever know what it was like without the experience itself.

I opened the letter from my soldier friend. He was stationed near Chicago and was having a gay time. He voiced disapproval of the way the civilian population in general were taking the war. They did not seem very serious about it, he said, and morals had become very loose, especially among the young women. That was something that I had not noticed. Of course, I had been very quickly trained and shipped out of the country. Perhaps things had changed, or maybe I hadn't been very observant. He ended the letter with a postscript—"Here is a newspaper clipping that may interest you."

I unfolded it and looked it over carefully. It contained a picture of Mary—my Mary. It also described a wedding ceremony. Mary was the girl I was to have married when I returned. She was now married to a deferred farmer.

I remembered the look on her face as I left my home town on the train. I saw it as if it had happened only yesterday. I remembered her exact words, "I'll wait right here for you until the day I die." The tears had streamed down her cheeks; now they were streaming down my own.

I turned the clipping over, for I had read no news for so long that any scrap would have interested me. It told of a young lady who had been arrested and fined ten dollars for disorderly conduct. She had been meeting and entertaining a German prisoner of war who was being used as a laborer in a cannery.

I gritted my teeth and read on. The next short article gave a brief account of an artillery shell factory that was on strike. The workmen were demanding better working conditions.

That did it. I felt a fit of rage trying to seize me. The enemy shells were still flying about, so I attempted to control myself.

I dug a small hole in the ground with my finger, stuffed the wadded clipping into it and covered it over with dirt. I took another look at the letter. The postscript stared back at me—"Here is a newspaper clipping that may interest you."

As I looked at it, the rain began again, causing the

ink to run. I was glad, for I did not want to read it again.

So they were striking in a shell factory for better working conditions? Each evening they could go to a fine home, sit with their families, and toast their shins while reading the evening paper by the fireplace. On this day I lay in the mud and slime in a gurgling field somewhere in France. I watched American soldiers die fighting seventy-five-ton steel monsters with bare hands and hand grenades, because of no artillery shells to fire at them. Our commanding officer had given the battle order for the day, "Death before dishonor; die rather than retreat." So they died, and their mothers would receive a telegram and a Purple Heart. They died for the lack of gasoline for our tanks and shells for our howitzers. Yes, I saw those shivering boys in the cold, driving rain, lying in the slimy ooze of mud and blood. Most of them had not been paid or had not had a good night of sleep in five or six months.

I suppose that very evening some strikebound civilian picked up the evening paper and remarked, "Well, I see we are still holding our own on the German front."

Lieutenant Ulman came running toward me in a low crouch, then flopped on his stomach beside my home. "How's your hand?" he asked.

"It's not too bad, although I know it isn't in the best of shape."

"Company C lost their last medic, and they need some help. You want to go over and lend a hand?"

I nodded my head, "Okay, I'll go over right now. I'll come back as soon as I can."

It was only about three hundred yards to Company

98

C, and the ground was covered with the fallen leaves of autumn. They were not the romantic rustling type that I had read about, but were cold and saturated with the penetrating rain. They stuck to everything that touched them.

As I made my way through the trees a bullet tore through my right thigh. It felt to me as if I had been pricked with a red hot needle. My knees buckled as another ripped through the palm of my right hand. It spun me part way around so I faced the enemy. As I continued downward, still a third hit my right thigh. My thigh being horizontal with the ground, it entered just inside the kneecap and came out on the inside, halfway to the crotch.

As I lay there on the ground I attempted to bandage myself. I wanted to work on my leg first, but it was impossible for it would have meant sitting up. I did the next best thing, tried to wrap my hand. I tried for several minutes, but got nowhere. Putting my face down in the wet leaves, the tears began to stream from my eyes. I had had enough. I had to leave the front; battle fatigue had overcome me. I could take it no longer.

I awoke with my back propped against a concrete pillbox. The tears were still wet on my face, and I was blubbering to myself. Lieutenant Ulman had his arm around my shoulders. He had seen me get hit and had carried me behind this pillbox. He had also cut off the right leg of my trousers and had dressed my wounds.

Handing me a shining silverlike bullet, he said, "Here, keep this as a souvenir. It's the slug that went from your knee through half the length of your thigh. I found it in your pants when I cut the leg off."

"Gee, thanks. Thanks a lot," I told him. "It certainly shines, doesn't it?"

"That's just the steel slug. The copper jacket is probably in your leg somewhere." He stood and adjusted his harness. "Well, so long and good luck. Hope to see you back soon."

He disappeared around the pillbox.

The litter bearers came, placed me on the litter, and I started the long, dreadful journey back.

V.

As I was carried back by the litter bearers I watched the golden brown trees of mid-October slide by. The winter only a short way off must be a terrible time on the front.

We passed the body of an enemy soldier apparently dead for several days for his skin was a greenish-black. The Americans seemed always to turn a blue-black. We had often talked about the Germans turning green. Some thought it was because of the food they ate, others, the locality from which they came. Still others blamed it on the tobacco they smoked. Usually a dead enemy soldier gave off a strong odor of tobacco similar to that of burning feathers or mildewed hay. What a blend they must have smoked!

The bridge across the river consisted of two steel troughs supported by dozens of rubber rafts. The shells that fell very freely were mostly mortar shells. The engineers were kept busy replacing the supporting rubber rafts for the shrapnel from the mortar shells punctured them.

As we passed over the river in one of the steel troughs, I looked down at the swirling water below. It was deep, dark, and treacherous looking. I breathed a prayer that nothing would happen to the litter bearers, for I did not want to be dropped into that cold, muddy water. Right then, I did not feel like swimming at all.

I wondered what the water could say if it could talk. A half mile upstream it was passing through enemy territory. Here it flowed through our small bridgehead and then on into enemy territory again. Here it had first washed against American-held territory—a small bridgehead beginning to crumble.

I made up the third casuality for an ambulance waiting on the river bank. We had to wait for one more as the shells burst about. Often the blast from an exploding shell rocked the ambulance. The driver asked us if we would like a cigarette. Only one fellow took one.

When the last casuality arrived we left. From the way the ambulance bounced, I could tell that we traveled cross-country through ditches and fields for quite some time.

We passed through several aid stations. At each one I was unloaded and after waiting in turn for several minutes a doctor peeked at my wounds and gave the order for me to be taken further on. Some places served hot coffee or cocoa, and sometimes we hardly had time to drink before we were loaded into another ambulance.

Finally I arrived at a field hospital set up in long, olive-drab tents. It was a beehive of activity, but no one was carrying a pack or wearing a helmet.

Before I had realized it the din of battle was gone. Even the distant booming of artillery had faded out. It was hard to believe, for during the past four and one-half months I had never been without that noise.

I had lived in constant fear of being hit by some piece of flying metal and I had never been able to walk unless in a crouch or without being on the constant lookout for the ever-present enemy.

The medical soldiers removed my clothing and put a pair of flannel pajamas on me. I was taken to one of the tents and placed on a cot of wood and canvas. Here there were no sheets, although there were two soft, warm, olive-drab blankets in addition to the one put over me.

Soon a nurse came with a basin of warm water, unbuttoned my pajama top, and bathed my face, arms, and chest. It felt good, ever so good—a warm, dry bed and warm water.

As the nurse leaned over me I looked at her clean, innocent-looking face. The eyes glowed softly and warmly, so different from any woman one might see at the front, so different from the staring eyes filled with fear and worry.

This was the first time since boyhood that a woman had bathed me. I lay in a stupor, staring at her soft, white face, but the warm water was the only thing that affected me. It made me tired, ever so tired. I tried to stay awake to realize as much of this scene as possible, but I could not.

I was jolted awake by the bouncing walk of two litter bearers. We had just entered the X-ray room.

The litter bearers lifted the stretcher and I was slid onto an X-ray table. They took a quick X-ray of each hand and of my right leg before I was placed back on the litter and lowered to the ground.

Within a few minutes they presented the litter

bearers with the films and once again we bounced to another tent, this time the operating tent. The powerful engine which generated the electricity roared incessantly. Several operating tables were lined up side by side in the ether-reeking shelter.

The lights over the operating table burned brightly over me and a medical soldier, dressed in white, appeared and removed my pajamas. I had nothing on except a pair of identification tags fastened about my neck with a beaded chain taped together with adhesive tape so they would not rattle. In England we had been ordered to do it. The tape was no longer white but black with the dirt, grime, and sweat of war. The medical soldier covered me with an army blanket.

A doctor appeared. He was young and handsome, but his face had none of the animation of most men of his age. He was stone-faced sober from the pain of seeing his countrymen torn, beaten, and mutilated.

For a moment he studied the X-ray films which the medical soldier had hung on a wire beside the table. Then with a pair of bandage scissors he cut the bandage from my left hand. It hurt and throbbed as he removed it, for it had been stuck to the wound. He looked it over closely.

"Can you move your fingers?" he asked.

I nodded my head and proceeded to wiggle them. It was painful, for my hand was swollen and sore.

After swabbing it with merthiolate he rebandaged it and used the same procedure on the other hand.

He bared my right leg by merely flipping the blanket over. His assistant removed the bandages as he alternated glances between my leg and the X-ray. Finally he turned and swabbed the entire wounded area with alcohol. Then, with a large, blunt, needlelike instrument, he pushed into the opening beside my kneecap. I tried to withdraw because of the pain, but his assistant anchored my leg firmly. I could feel the instrument being inched up into the wound as beads of sweat appeared on my upper lip and forehead. When it got into the fleshy part, just above the knee, I felt it strike something. It ticked two or three times, as if hitting metal, then was withdrawn. I tried to lie perfectly still, breathing very hard.

A needle pricked me sharply as a local anesthetic was injected. A few moments passed before the job was resumed, then I could feel the movements and hear the ticking again as his instruments touched the piece of metal in my leg.

Finally it was removed. The doctor rinsed it off and handed it to me, then walked away, removing his gloves as he went. The assistant wrapped my leg. Just as Lieutenant Ulman had told me, it was the copper jacket from the German bullet. It had been split open and was very jagged.

My pajamas were replaced and the litter bearers were called.

As we passed through the outdoors, between tents, I looked up at the black, rolling skies above. It was black, ever so black all about, but there was no roar of battle to fill the night. The odor of fall was here and winter was not too far off. I asked the time of one of the litter bearers.

"One thirty," he grunted.

I was placed back on the cot and covered. I was now

ready for a nice, long sleep that would remove some of the creases from my face and the pink from my eyeballs. But before I could close my eyes the nurse came up with a handful of sulfa pills and a glass of water.

"Here, take these," she whispered.

"All of those?" I protested, pointing to the handful of pills.

"Yes."

"But I'm not that sick."

"Take them and be quiet so you don't wake the others," she ordered.

I jammed them into my mouth, chewed them a bit, and then tried to wash them down by guzzling the water. She stayed to make sure that I did not spit them out.

As she left, a medical soldier came with a hypodermic.

"Turn over," he ordered.

"What do you have there?" I demanded as I turned over on my stomach.

"Penicillin."

He pulled my pajamas down, jabbed me in the buttocks, replaced my pajamas and blanket, then disappeared.

At once I fell into a deep sleep. Throughout the night I was awakened several times and jabbed in the buttocks. It did not fully awaken me each time, but by morning I realized that I had had several shots. The memory of them was quite hazy, for my sleep was so sound. Never before had I ever slept that soundly.

I was shaken awake to find a soldier standing over me

holding a steel tray with my breakfast. When I sat up and he placed it on my lap, I looked at it for a moment. Scrambled eggs, fried potatoes, and a cup of coffee. The sulfa pills had made my stomach quite upset, but I thought that perhaps the food would settle my stomach.

During the morning I was still given shots in the buttocks. I tried to sleep, but I could not. Things were too nice and peaceful here—no booming from artillery, no rattling from the machine gun, no stench from burning, dying cities.

A nurse came with a basin of hot water, a safety razor, and some soap. The way she shaved me made me think that she had done it often. It pulled a bit because my beard was a bit longer than was good for shaving, but when she had finished she washed my face and I felt clean, ever so clean. My face felt good, but naked.

Shortly after lunch, the litter bearers pulled up alongside my cot. I was slid onto it, taken out, and placed in an ambulance. The ride was a short one, and before long I was loaded aboard a hospital train.

The sheets on the bed felt cold at first. They were crisp, and they smelled clean. I felt great. A nice bed, clean sheets, clean pajamas. I felt so good I could have shouted or maybe cried—I could not tell exactly which.

We passed through town after town—a lot of meaningless names. Often we had to stop and wait for another train which was coming and must pass. Then the little train jerked onward once again, its squeaky whistle screaming girlishly.

The train skirted Paris and then headed west once again. By this time I had been given all the penicillin shots required, and I was glad, for my seat was getting quite sore from having been jabbed so often—fifteen times in all. The fellow in the bed across the aisle remarked, "You look like you've been hit in the rump with a burp gun."

The next morning during breakfast I heard several comments regarding a negro located two beds down the aisle from me. He was a quartermaster truck driver who had been involved in a wreck and had a severe gash in his left forearm. Now it had broken open and was hemorrhaging.

Several of the fellows gave the young negro suggestions. A nurse came by, and she was told about it. She looked at him for a moment, then scurried off. A young major came past, and one of the fellows stopped him and pointed out the colored youth. He glanced at him and continued on.

A quarter of an hour passed. The color began to fade from the negro's face, and the dressing on his arm was saturated with warm, red blood which flowed out onto the bedding. I sat up in my bed to make sure that I was seeing an American soldier bleeding to death beneath the very noses of the doctors and nurses sent to save him. I could not understand it. Maybe it was I; perhaps I was seeing wrong. This battle fatigue must be worse than I realized.

I stood up in the aisle, and my right leg nearly buckled beneath me as I made my way to the colored man's bed. "What's wrong with that doctor? Why didn't he tend to you?" I muttered.

He looked up at me with the softest, most appealing look that I had yet witnessed in a man's face. His eyes were mousy—like black beads in his head. They pleaded for help. They seemed to cry without tears. "He's a Southern gentleman and don't care to work much for us colored boys."

"Hell!" I blurted.

With as much tenderness as my bandaged hands would permit, I pulled apart a couple of turns of the bandage. Pushing the dressing as far aside as I could, I saw that an artery was spurting from somewhere deep in the wide jellylike wound. With the thumb and fore-finger of my right hand, I pushed deep into the surging, scarlet mass of half-clotted blood. Finding the slippery end of the severed artery, I clamped it tightly with my thumb and finger. The negro flinched slightly but looked relieved as he watched the spurting stop.

After awhile the major reappeared in the car. I stood defiantly in the aisle; I would stop him this time. If he refused, I would notify the Inspector General's Depart-ment. Right was right, regardless.

He stamped up before me. He looked at the negro and then at me.

"Get back to your bed, soldier," he ordered. "I'll take care of this."

I hobbled back to my bed, feeling browbeaten and very sheepish. I did not know whether I had done the right or the wrong thing. I could only remember the look upon the face of the paling negro. I would be glad to leave the train.

By evening the train pulled into the seaport of Cher-bourg. It was a bustling little place with many unshaded electric lights showing the dozens of cranes there to un-load the precious cargoes from across the ocean.

Hardly had the train stopped than I was loaded onto a litter and taken out. I was among the first to go. I liked it better than the waiting and wondering one goes through when he is among the last to be taken.

As I was carried past the negro whom I had helped he clasped my hand warmly, "Thanks, friend, and you are a friend. I'll never forget you."

A short ambulance ride into the country brought us to a large general hospital set up in tents and covering several acres among the small hedgerowed fields. The hedgerows looked inviting and good for a change. It had been several months since I had been in this territory. It was something like coming home—coming back to a place that I had been familiar with, even though there was not a soul whom I may know.

A soldier's utmost desire is to go home, to go to a place where he is familiar with the terrain as well as the people. He fights a war with this uppermost in his mind. Every day he is on the front is one more day nearer to the time he will be home. Every mile he walks is one more mile closer to home, though it be in the opposite direction. He thinks of this early and often; he believes it and lives it, even when the odds are a thousand to one against his living another minute. After many weeks and months of battle the real picture of home fades and becomes distorted. Anything that comes near this hope is stretched to fit it. Coming back to the hedgerow country of Normandy gave me as much of a tingle as when I had received my first furlough.

Life in a general hospital seemed wonderful to a combat man, especially when he had nothing more wrong with him than I had. I was severely wounded, but nothing vital had been injured. Time and care would heal me completely.

Each morning I was awakened by a gentle tug at my pajama sleeve. Meals were brought in on trays. They were wholesome and satisfying; so different from the cheese and chocolate of the combat rations. With the sudden change of diet and the abundance of sleep that I now received I should have become fat before long.

Within a few days I was caught up on my sleep and much of the soreness had left the area of my wounds. Even the soreness in my seat from the penicillin shots had gone. I decided that I must write a letter home—a letter that would ease some of the torture caused by the telegram the War Department sent to my mother when I was wounded.

That afternoon the nurse led a Red Cross lady to my bed.

"The nurse tells me you would like to send a letter home, so I came to give you a hand. Is that all right by you?"

"Sure, that's wonderful," I replied.

I told her a few things to write, and she filled in the rest. It was nothing personal, for I could not tell anyone of personal matters; I was too bashful. Not only she, but also the fellows on each side, would have heard. She wrote that my hands were injured, and that she, a Red Cross worker, was writing for me. If this had not been explained, it would only have caused more grief to my mother, for she would have known instantly that I had not written this letter.

By the tenth day I was able to get out of bed and hop

about the ward. Long hours of the day were often spent playing cards on the beds of some of the other fellows, but now I even ventured out to the latrine tent, set up a few feet behind the ward.

Afternoons in the ward became very warm because of heat rays from the bright, autumn sun. The crisp fall air invited me to go out and stroll about.

My first problem was to get some clothing besides the flannel pajamas. After a short talk with my nurse, low-toned talk, she agreed to get me a complete outfit. She took the sizes down on a piece of paper.

My new issue of clothing enabled me to go to the Red Cross tent and read various papers and magazines, attend a movie in the evening, and eat my meals in a mess tent.

At first I had to hobble about or walk only short distances, but soon I could go for longer walks and I limped only slightly. It was much better than lying on one's back in a hot tent, listening to other soldiers arguing over the many battles of the war. Most of those who debated were not real front-line soldiers. The combat soldier talked of the war very little and thought long and very deeply. News was no longer news to him. He cared not who had won the battles nor who had received the credit for it. He only knew that he was doing his part.

One afternoon I decided to go for a walk out into the countryside. It was against regulations, so I told no one. The last field before leaving the hospital area was an orchard, and the apples were the golden yellow of full ripeness. They were small and hard—used chiefly in the making of cider and other drinks. I pushed half a dozen into my pockets, then went out onto the narrow dirt road which lay across the next fence.

As I walked slowly down the dusty road, I could see many pieces of enemy equipment in the fields and ditches. I stopped to examine a light machine gun which lay beside the road. It still had its steel belt of live ammunition threaded through it. The wooden stock was gray, cracked, and weatherbeaten. The entire steel portion was rusty—so rusty that none of the parts would move. It was different from those that I had been used to seeing—so bright, shiny, and well oiled. Often I had been afraid to pick one up for fear of its firing, but as I looked this rusty piece of equipment over, I was sure that it would never fire again. It was as dead as all defeated weapons should be.

A few hundred yards farther on I came upon a small village with a Catholic church whose windows had been shattered and blown out. The entire yard surrounding the church was filled with tombstones of all descriptions. I remembered then that most of the church yards in Normandy were the burial ground of the faithful. This one was quiet and peaceful now. The roar of battle had passed on, and the tombstones could go on rotting once again.

Across the street a black, unpainted house loomed. Tall shrubs and vines lined the short path to the stairs which led to the front door. On the door, painted in gold letters, was the word "Maire." It certainly was not much of a house for an official to occupy, but perhaps poor people had poor means. In the United States a settlement of this size would not have been incorporated.

Walking on to a fork in the road, I saw a small place

of business described by a sign, "Epicerie—Cidre." I was interested in the latter, for it was pronounced "cedar," but in the American language it was just plain cider—apple juice.

As I entered the door two other soldiers, wearing field jackets and helmet liners, left the place. It looked more like a well worn, rustic tavern, with small round tables and an assortment of wooden, wire, and wicker chairs. Apparently the business had grown tremendously in the last few months, and the only furniture he could obtain were these dilapidated pieces from the surrounding community. The keeper himself was a small, dark-complexioned man who eyed me suspiciously. I could see his plump wife and young boy in a back room.

On a table he had several gallon jugs of cider. I looked them over, picked one up, and petted it. The Frenchman came over to my side, so I licked my lips with my tongue in order that he could see it. After setting it down again, I reached into my brand-new pockets, empty except for a couple of small, hard apples. I turned my pockets inside out to make the Frenchman understand that I had no money.

He understood and poured a glass for me. It did not taste nearly so rich and flavorful as that I used to get at home, but it was good. It had been a long time since I had had any to drink.

I stood, sipping at the cider, staring out the window. Lying in the ditch across the road was the broken barrel of a German eighty-eight. The bright-colored leaves of autumn were strewn about the ground. This brilliance of fall got me into its spell of enchantment, so I gulped down the cider, thanked the proprietor, and departed without hesitation. I wanted to get closer to nature in the woods and fields, so that I could be alone.

I passed through a muddle of some half dozen haphazardly strewn homes and on down another winding dirt road. A footpath turned to the left, so I took it. It had been carpeted with thousands of fallen leaves, and as I padded along, watching the leaves shuffling before my heavily shod feet, I thought of the years that nature must have worked to create such a cushion upon the face of the earth. Scraping away the bright-colored leaves, I could see the dark brown ones from the last year, and the wet, half decayed ones from the year before, and so on to the very soil. It was dark, damp, and rich with a peculiar odor of its own.

Down the path lay a small pond of still, dirty water with ducks swimming at one end, while a tomato-faced French woman washed clothes at the other.

I stopped for a moment to watch her, but she did not even look up. She knelt on a large, flat rock that extended out into the water, her wooden shoes resting on the bank behind her. They were cushioned with loose, dried grass for she wore no stockings.

After dipping a garment into the brown water, she wadded it up on the rock and beat it with a small wooden paddle. She repeated the process time and again. After hours of hard work, her laundry was still dirtier than that of the average American housewife before she washes.

A few towering pines, a lone poppy, and the afternoon sun. What a wonderful, peaceful spot after the hell, rain, and torture of the front! I could have stayed forever.

I headed back toward the hospital, making a large arc through the hedgerowed fields. My right thigh was beginning to throb a bit; it had had enough exercise for one day.

Within view of the hospital grounds, I came upon a rusty row of entanglements. Farther on I could see three huge mounds of earth which looked out of the ordinary for this part of the country. Investigation revealed that they were concrete pillboxes covered with earth.

The first was about twenty feet high, and twenty-five feet in diameter on the inside. Except for its heavy steel doors, the entire concrete fortification was covered with grassy earth so that it must have been invisible from the air. Its heavy, wooden-wheeled howitzer had been pulled out and set up in the rear. Apparently things had not happened as the Germans had planned and they found they had to fight the Americans from the rear rather than from the direction of the sea. Instead of having a concrete cover, they had to bring the howitzer out into the open field.

Huge stacks of one hundred and fifty-five-millimeter shells lay in pits, under trees, and in the pillboxes. Large quantities of land mines, grenades, and small-arms ammunition were stored in the pillbox.

The hospital spread out before me, a pillbox to the right and left and an orchard behind. I could not see the ocean, but I knew that it lay two or three miles beyond. The howitzer had been pointed straight toward it when it was inside the fortification.

The next afternoon found me strolling down the same dusty, crooked road that I had taken the day before. This time I traveled in the opposite direction. At the first farm that I came to, some soldiers were bartering with a husky, young Norman maiden, trading chewing gum and cigarettes for straw. They could use it in their pup tents to ward off the damp chill of the gurgling soil.

The little dirt road soon wound its way to a well-used macadam highway. In the ditch at the intersection sat a fifty-millimeter defense gun, well imbedded in an open concrete fortification. At this point, the highway descended down a long hill into the very heart of the port of Cherbourg. This was a wonderful defensive position.

The only trouble with this weapon, as well as most of the other coastal installations, was that it could not be turned around. In this sector, as well as at nearly all other places on the coast, the Americans had come from the rear.

A few yards away a huge brick tower, built like a lighthouse, overlooked the countryside. Inside, a steel spiral stairway made its way to the top. I tried climbing it, but my leg gave out on the first few steps.

Looking down the highway into Cherbourg gave me a longing to go there, but I looked back at the tower and remembered my leg.

Turning, I slowly made my way back toward the hospital once again.

As I walked down the concrete aisle, past loaded litters just brought in, I stopped in amazement. There, in one of them, lay one of my buddies from Company H. His name was Fillmore.

Kneeling beside him, I shook his hand. His face lit up, and his eyes sparkled. How wonderful it was to find someone among all these men that I knew. Then I realized that this was a hospital, not a city park. Soldiers didn't come here for a visit, especially when they were carried in.

"What's wrong? Where did you get it?" I blurted.

"I didn't get hit. It's trenchfoot from lying in cold water in those filthy pillboxes across the river."

"So they drove you back to the pillboxes?" I asked.

"Not only to the pillboxes, but clean back across the river. The bridgehead is a thing of the past."

"How long did you hold the pillboxes?"

"I don't know. Seven of us were in the one where I was. For four days we stood, sat, and lay, in two feet of cold water. Then we had to get out and go back across the river. That was the real nightmare. It was then that my feet began to burn. Now they are swollen and so sore that I can't touch them."

I looked down at his feet. The blanket was rolled back to his shins, and his shiny, swollen feet protruded.

I pointed out my bed and told him that I'd be back to see him when he had been cleared through all the red tape. Then I went to my bed.

After lunch, I stopped at his litter for another little chat. He had been fed, and his tray rested on the floor beside him.

"How do you go about getting a bed here?" he asked.

"Oh, they'll have one for you in a day or two," I assured him. "Some of these fellows are due to be shipped out soon."

"Where do they go from here?"

"Well, if you cannot be healed, or if it takes more than thirty days to cure you, they will send you to the

U. K. For anything less than that, you will stay here until you're well, and then back to the line you go."

"What's U. K. stand for?"

"United Kingdom."

The next morning, immediately after breakfast, I left the hospital area. Proceeding back to the highway, I began hitch-hiking. A colored quartermaster driver gave me a ride in an army six by six. As I sat in the cab of the truck, watching the many small fields whizz by, I realized that it was my first ride like this in many, many months. I could not recall how long it had been since I had driven a motor vehicle. The driver watched this endless road come up before him and his head bounced up and down as we jarred along. Neither of us spoke. We didn't have to. There was no news, for it was still the same old story that had been going on for so long. He didn't even ask where I was going.

As we approached the small village of Ste. Mere Eglise, I could see something white gleaming through the trees about a half mile away. At first it looked like snow, but soon I could make it out—a military cemetery. When we got into the village, I asked the driver to drop me off.

A narrow dirt road wound its way in the direction of the cemetery. In the fields on both the right and left were the remains of the gliders which had brought the first wave of the airborne invasion. Probably many of those invaders lay in that cemetery. A few of the fields had huge posts standing upright and spaced to prevent a glider from being able to land without crashing. They had been imported to this area, for nowhere over here had I seen trees of this type and size.

Turning, I got back on the road and followed it a short distance to the farmhouse at its end. A stocky Frenchman, wearing a cap, came out to greet me. His dark hair and bushy mustache turning gray made him look about the age to have been in the last war.

Beckoning me into a junk-filled woodshed adjoining his home, he handed me a glass of strong cider. We sat on blocks of wood and sipped it. His rosy cheeks led me to think that he had consumed a lot of it.

He talked to me a long time in a language which I did not understand, but I listened attentively, as if I did. Soon he jumped up and dramatically explained that he had been a soldier in the last war. Rolling up his left sleeve, he uncovered a huge scar—two inches wide and eight inches long on each side of his shrunken bicep. His gesture revealed that a German had bayonetted him in the last war. "Boche! Ah, Boche!" he spat out between times. Then he pulled a burlap bag from the rafters and a camouflaged nylon parachute and a red supply chute rolled out. "American!" he explained.

As I fingered the parachutes he brought out a small black address book. As I opened it he gestured that this address book had come from the soldier who had used this parachute. He had landed in the pasture which lay just across the fence and was killed either before he had landed or shortly afterward. I could not understand just which it was.

Looking into the book, I saw the name and home address of an old buddy of mine. We had gone to school together. He was one of the fellows that I had read about in the newspaper clipping that Mother had sent to me. So that's the way Walter had died? There lay the field that he had given his life to liberate. I wondered if this Frenchman really appreciated this fact.

I asked him where Walter was now. He pointed in the direction of the cemetery.

He drew another glass of cider and invited me into his house to show me his discharge certificate from the French army. From his awards I gathered that he must have been a brave soldier.

Bringing forth a large book, he showed me his marriage certificate and the birth certificates of his children.

"Where are they?" I asked.

He seemed to understand. Shrugging his shoulders, he showed me that they had been taken away. "Boche!" he growled.

Tears came into his eyes, and I bowed my head to show that I wished to share his sorrow.

Returning to the cemetery, I went into the office and gave them the names of three friends that Mother told me had been killed over here. They had only two of them.

The cemetery was divided into square plots of graves. The plots were lettered, and the graves were numbered. I found the first one—plot B, grave 148. I left the gravel path and walked across the gray mounds between the crosses, until I came to a white cross. On the crosspiece, in black, was the name and serial number. On the bottom of the upright portion of the cross, just above the earth, was the number 148. On the other side was tacked on his identification tag. The other must have been on the body.

After finding the other grave I wandered about and

looked the place over. Rank made no difference here. A major lay beside a private, a Jew beside a Gentile. Sex made no difference either. Many of the heroes were unknown, and I wondered if the army would ever find out who they were? The graves in the last few plots were sunken and broken, for the earth had not had time to settle. A few broken gliders lay about the hedgerow that surrounded the area. The holes and trenches along this hedgerow had apparently been dug by the men who had come into this foreign field by those gliders.

As I made my way back toward the gateway, I passed the tall steel pole from which a bright American flag whipped in the breeze. At its base lay many bouquets of flowers. They seemed to be there in answer to the question that I had asked myself an hour or so before. Yes, the Frenchmen did appreciate the fact that these men had given their lives to make them free once again. With this in mind, I left the Blosville Cemetery of Ste. Mere Eglise—the first area and village liberated by the Americans.

Another truck took me into Cherbourg. I got out at the busy dock section, where a canal came up and into the city. Dozens of vessels, mostly from England, were unloading fuel and supplies. Heavy American trucks were being loaded to capacity and over. The large red circle painted on their front meant that many belonged to a general's famous "Red Ball" truck line. They were to have road priority over most other vehicles so, as one colored driver expressed it, they could get to the front "firstest with the mostest."

I came upon a bit of activity near one of the ships being unloaded. They had just pulled a human body up and onto the dock. A diver was in the process of being hauled up. The body was badly decomposed, dismembered, and without clothing. One could not tell the sex or nationality of this mass of bone and tissue. One of the arms had been stretched to twice its normal length.

"What happened to him?" I asked one of the fellows helping on this detail.

"He was tangled in the screws of this ship," he replied.

"This must be a rare sight."

"Rare nothing. It's a full time job for us."

"Where do they all come from, and who are they?" I asked.

"They're French, English, and American soldiers, with a few civilians in between. The entire invasion coast is full of them. Been there since D-day."

I pumped him for more information, "How come they leave them there?"

"Why, hell, Joe, the entire area is full of mines." He raised his voice with impatience. "You'll learn after you've been over here another week."

"Thanks. Thanks a lot," I told him. I had an urge to push him into the canal, but I controlled myself. If I got into trouble while being away from the hospital without permission, I would really have been in trouble. I walked away, grumbling to myself. Yes, I knew that the coast was mined. I had found out the hard way. I wondered if the wounded soldier I had tried to pull ashore was still out there floating among the mines and beach obstacles? Perhaps it was he they had just unwound from the screws of the vessel.

123

Before I could get to a Red Cross canteen, two M. P.'s stopped me because I had no leggings. I also was supposed to wear either a helmet liner or a necktie. Humbly, I told them that I was sorry, that I didn't know about the regulation. They were very understanding, too understanding. I was sure they knew just about what my situation was.

"We'll let you go this time," one of them told me, "but watch it."

The canteen had a tremendous number of soldiers and sailors waiting in line for coffee and doughnuts. I fell in and silently waited my turn. When I came up to the young French server she refused me, for I did not have coupons for my coffee and doughnuts. I gave her an argument, but she ignored me and passed them to the soldier behind me. I turned to him.

"What's this all about?" I asked.

"You have to buy a ticket of coupons from that booth in the center of the floor."

"Buy!" I shouted. "This is the American Red Cross, isn't it? That's army coffee and flour, cooked and served with French help, isn't it? What kind of a racket is this?"

Placing my hands on my hips, I continued, "I waded ashore, mister; I didn't walk down a gangplank. I haven't been paid in five months."

My temples throbbed and I trembled from head to foot. I felt like breaking everything apart.

He handed me a twenty-franc note, "Here, I'll give you this. If you need more, let me know."

I purchased a ticket and waited my turn in line again. When I reached the counter, two naval officers came rushing up and presented their coupons. The server told them to get in line and wait their turn.

"*Officier! Officier!*" they protested in broken French, pointing to their insignia.

She ignored them and continued to serve the line. Most of the soldiers in line gave them a hearty laugh and sneer as they turned and retreated out the door.

After getting a cup of coffee and two doughnuts I went out the door and looked up and down the streets at the milling crowd of soldiers and civilians. Then I remembered the M. P.'s. In the same thought, I remembered the steep hill which I must climb to get out of Cherbourg. Quickly, I struck out in the direction from which I had come.

Once again I was stopped by the Military Police. It was a different pair than had stopped me before, but they gave me the routine and let me go.

The bridge across the canal was open, so I had to wait. A small tug passed through before the bridge went down. An army six by six was waiting to cross, so I opened the flap on the canvas door.

"Going my way, out of town?" I asked, pointing in the general direction.

"Sure, jump in," he answered.

I jumped in, and we were off. It was easy for a soldier to get a ride over here. The truck was loaded with cans of water to take to his organization. All water had to come from an army water point, for there it was run through a purifier. The army would not permit soldiers to drink water that had not been purified.

As we were leaving the outskirts of the city a funeral procession came down the road. It was led by a priest who held a long cross before him. The black-draped casket was carried by four men wearing silk tophats, and a trail of mourners followed behind. The very impressive ceremony was ever so slow on our modern highways of today.

A bit farther, we climbed the long, black ribbon of highway up the mighty hill. Part way up, we saw a large army semi-truck going out of control. We stopped to await the outcome as the large truck swerved madly about the highway a great distance from us. There was a possibility that it could continue this far.

Soon it went completely out of control and left the highway, piling into a concrete telephone pole. I could see the driver's head tear through the canvas top of the cab. As it did, the broken concrete pole crashed down on it, as if to knock the driver back into his seat. In flying forward his neck fell directly over the framework about the windshield, and the pole forced it to cleave through like a guillotine. The head rolled off the front of the truck and into the ditch, while his body slumped down into the seat.

Braking our truck, we jumped out and ran up to the wreck, but there was nothing we could do. The eyes on the head in the ditch still blinked feebly. The blood from the body flowed over the running board and down into the ditch.

A French woman rushed over and placed a bouquet of flowers on the chest of the beheaded driver. As she wept she told us that her son had died in the French army in the same manner. It was in 1940, when the Germans came in. Then she knelt and began to pray.

It was nearly dark by the time I got back to the hospital, but I managed to get in on the tail end of the chow line. They had run out of the good ham, so I had to eat the substitute—corned beef hash.

Back in the ward, I lay upon my bed with my clothing on. I had removed my shoes. The fellow in the next bed offered me a cigar. I did not usually smoke, but I accepted it to give me something to while away the time.

I watched the thin blue smoke curl lazily upwards. I knew better than to inhale, so I puffed at it leisurely and blew an occasional smoke ring. My eyes stared at the tent roof, but I did not see it. I saw the fields of Normandy, the rows of white crosses, and the quivering body of the beheaded soldier of the Quartermaster Corps.

A soldier's voice broke the silence of the ward, "Movie tonight in the recreation tent. That's right next to the mess tent. It starts at seven-thirty."

Apparently he was one of the medical soldiers who had been sent to inform all the wards, for he was dressed in neatly laundered fatigues.

Before he could turn to depart, he was bombarded with a dozen questions.

"How much?"

"Any special uniform?"

"What's playing?"

I slipped on my shoes and went over immediately in anticipation of a good seat. When I got there, there was standing room only. The screen was near the other end of the tent. It was a portable screen, set up six or eight feet from the opposite wall. I went behind it and sat on the floor with my back against the wall. The only difference in seeing the picture from this side would be in reading matter—it would appear backward. I could well afford to miss that.

A few days later I was given notice that I was to be shipped out the following day. Most of the day was to be spent obtaining clothing and equipment and getting it ready to travel.

I got a complete new outfit. Most of the extra clothing and equipment I tried to talk the quartermaster into keeping, but it did no good, so I staggered away under a load three times larger than needed.

Cushion-soled socks and combat boots were the things I prized most—warmth for my feet for the coming winter, and no bothersome leggings to come undone and trip me.

I looked up Fillmore—the fellow from my outfit. When I found him, he was in another ward, lying in a bed, staring at the roof of the tent. His swollen feet still protruded at the foot of the bed. They rested even higher now, on a pillow. They were turning black, and I could scent a faint odor common only to dead flesh. He seemed a bit depressed.

"Hi, Fillmore, old boy!" I tried to brighten him up. "How are you doing today?"

I sat on the edge of the bed.

"Oh, hello, Doc." He faked a smile. "Getting along all right so far. How's things with you?"

"I'm doing all right for myself too—leaving tomorrow."

We soon ran out of things to talk about, so we just sat and stared—he at the roof and I down at the aisle.

A nurse came in and placed a towel under his feet and applied a mineral oil to them.

"What does that do?" I asked.

"It keeps them from cracking and splitting," she answered.

"Sure feels good," Fillmore added.

After she left, I still stared at his feet. They must be amputated; I knew that. It was only a matter of time. He knew it too. Neither of us would admit it or talk about it.

"When are you going to go to a dance?" I asked with a smile.

"By Christmas, I hope," he answered.

VI.

A SIX-BY-SIX truck whined its way through the cold, dark, November morning, taking us into still sleeping Cherbourg. The bright stars managed to get their last few blinks in before the rising sun. We huddled silently together in the open truck.

The barracks of an airfield was our next home. It was cold and the wind blew in and moaned through the shattered windows. I tossed my equipment into a corner and turned back to the field.

The field overlooked the gray sea of foaming white-caps glittering in the rising sun. A wrecked C-47 transport plane rested in a pile at one side. A huge Indian, with the word "Geronimo" in hideous yellow, decorated its dull nose. For a moment I stood and stared at it, wondering what history it held. Why was it there? What had happened to the crew?

I strolled out on the huge concrete breakwater which sheltered the harbor. Wrecked vessels littered its sides, and smelly fishing boats rested at anchor in between. Out in the harbor a few tugs grunted about among the large steamers snoozing between voyages.

Soon I discovered that what I was walking on not only was an ordinary breakwater but a huge, deep fortification. Tons of ammunition and supplies jammed its interior in disorderly fashion.

A biting sea wind drove me back toward the airfield. On the way I passed a few wrecked enemy planes. My! They must have had troops and equipment scattered over a tremendous area. How did such a small nation ever accomplish so much with so little?

After stuffing my stomach with hot stew I returned to the shattered barracks in which I was to sleep. The days were getting short now, for already it was quite dark.

Someone had found an old stove, so we made a fire and huddled around it. There was no stovepipe, but the smoke rose and went out the broken windows, while the flame spouted from the opening, making weird shadows which danced about on the brick walls.

In a far corner I could see that a card game was getting under way. For light they used a piece of tent rope pushed into a can of shoe grease.

I lay down on a canvas cot and watched the shadows dance on the ceiling while the chatter of my comrades buzzed in my ears.

Seventeen of us were jammed into a small, four-wheeled box car. Our equipment, stacked at one end, took up half of the car. A case of rations was to keep us until we arrived at our destination.

Once again I heard the coughing of a struggling locomotive, its shrieking female whistle cracking through the crisp November air. This cargo of American youth was being carried to the cold, grim front. I wondered how many had roundtrip tickets?

At one point along the way the train slowed to a

creeping pace, for a new section of track had been laid on soft, fresh dirt. A bulldozer was pushing more earth along the sides of the track, occasionally scooping up a five-hundred-pound bomb from the depths of the new soil.

Far out in a field bent frames and scattered wheels gave grim testimony of what had happened to an ammunition train that got this far. Beyond the crater of churned earth the blackened weeds and grass were blown flat. A fence had disappeared completely. For five hundred yards nothing was left standing and beyond that the scattered remains of the train rested.

As we passed through the dozens of war-scarred villages small bands of natives cheered and waved to us. Many of them tried to hand us parcels, but the train moved on too rapidly.

At one place, however, a bearded Frenchman managed to get a bottle to us. It had no label, but one of the fellows took a smell and yelled, "Calvados!"

As it was passed around for each of us to take a drink, the powerful odor nearly caused me to sneeze, but a strong combat man could not turn his head on something like this. What would the others have thought? I put the bottle to my lips, made one speedy gulp, and passed it on. Immediately I felt seared to the very pit of my stomach. It tasted like raw alcohol, tainted with some type of petroleum.

At night we tried to go to sleep, but it was too cold, and the train jerked too often. I had not been thoroughly warm since the last night in the hospital bed.

At one point the train stopped. I saw a stove in a shack beside the tracks, so one of my comrades and I got it into the boxcar. I grabbed some stovepipe and coal.

We set the stove up and stuck the pipe out the partly opened door. With the ration box we built a fire. Soon the smoke became so thick that breathing was difficult. After adding a bit of coal, we were forced to open the door wide and push the stove out. I watched the fiery coals disappear into the darkness behind as a falling snow began to blanket the countryside.

After another two days on the cold, bumpy train, we arrived at our destination. It was a town a short distance north of Paris that had felt the brunt of two world wars. We were herded into another old French army camp, surrounded by watch towers and a high, double fence filled with barbed wire entanglements. It must have served as a concentration camp during the days of the German occupation.

The room in the building in which our group was to stay was cold and damp. Most of the glass still remained in the windows, but there had been no heat for a long time. Double bunkbeds of rough slabwood lined each side of the walls, but there were no mattresses. A small stove with a long, leaning stovepipe sat in the center of the room.

I grabbed an upper bunk a few beds from the door, while a fellow named Charley Kruse took the lower portion of it. He was a blonde fellow of medium build from Chattanooga who had been in England for the past fifteen months serving in the Quartermaster Corps.

"What are you doing here?" I questioned him.

"Beats me. Just being transferred to another outfit."

We finished unrolling our blankets across the rough slats which made up the bottom of the beds.

"Let's get some wood and get that stove going," I suggested.

"I'm with you," he said, slapping on his helmet as he started for the door.

We searched for half an hour, but not a scrap of wood could we find, for apparently those before us had picked up the few remaining pieces. Even the near-by forest had been cleaned thoroughly of everything except the large trees.

Returning to the cold barracks with no wood for a fire made us feel rather down in the mouth. The others had gone to supper, so Charley and I got the mess kits from our packs, and headed for the mess hall, as a light snow began to fall.

It was a small brick building, with a greasy smell and large kettles of German manufacture sitting about the wet concrete. As we walked through, the food was ladled out in large gobs. There was no place to sit to eat, so we stood or squatted on our haunches against the outside of the building.

I watched the falling snowflakes dissolve as they landed in my steaming cup of coffee. A sudden gust of wind sprinkled the beans with sand, but I wolfed them down anyway.

The barracks grew increasingly colder as the snow-storm began in earnest. We stood about the cold stove with our blankets wrapped about us Indian fashion, telling jokes and talking in general. A single light bulb hung above. One could nearly count the low cycle as it blinked weakly on.

As I watched the bulb I wondered what would hap-

134

pen if it should burn out. Would we ever be able to find another? I worried about too many things. The world wouldn't stop turning if this light was to become broken or burnt out. I must let things take their course.

I was jarred from my daydream by the question of a fellow roommate, "Do you have any tent pins or poles?"

I looked down at the armful he had already collected, then took them from my pack and brought them over to the stove where a fire already crackled. What a bunch of soldiers wouldn't do to make their miserable conditions a bit more comfortable!

"Sure burns good," someone remarked.

"Yah! Wait until we get our next equipment check," a burly redhead added. "We'll pay for it."

Everyone chuckled a bit.

In the morning we had to stand in snow a foot deep just outside the barracks to answer the roll call. A sergeant called off the last name, and each soldier had to answer back with his first name and middle initial.

When it was over we were ordered to return to our rooms and lay our clothing and equipment out on the beds. It was a check to determine the shortages some of the soldiers may have.

"I guess the tent peg shortage is pretty acute here," Charley mused.

"Don't worry about those," I assured him. "You'll never need them."

The inspecting lieutenant came to my bed. After he glanced over my layout he turned to the sergeant following him and barked, "Short one rifle."

135

The sergeant wrote it down.

"But, sir," I interrupted. "I'm a medical soldier."

"You were a medical soldier," he snapped back. "You're an infantry rifleman now."

I gulped in amazement. My skin became like gooseflesh.

"I, Frank, a rifleman?" I asked myself. What had I done to warrant this? A lowly, mud-slogging dogface. Perhaps God had remembered the two enemy soldiers that I had slain back in Normandy. Now it would be legal for me to do so. Now I had to fight for my life. I had to kill or be killed.

When the lieutenant had finished the inspection and returned to the door he turned to us and gave a resume of why we were there and what we were to do.

We were all infantrymen, needed to fill the gaps in the ranks at the front. Replacements had not been coming over from the United States fast enough to maintain the ever-broadening front. He went on to tell us that we had suffered two thousand casualties a day during the invasion and at this time it was but fifteen hundred.

"That is a lot of replacements to burn up each day," he said with a gesture of the hand.

"Can we get a pass during our stay here?" a cool-eyed engineer asked.

"No soap!" the lieutenant snapped. "You'll be here about two weeks. In those two weeks you're going to figure out which end of the rifle you put to your shoulder and where to duck when the screaming mimis drop in on you."

He removed his helmet and scratched his bristling

head. "How long has it been since you've had one?" he asked with one eye shut.

"Since July of forty-one," answered the engineer coolly.

"Where have you been since then?" questioned the lieutenant.

"Iceland," the engineer replied drearily.

"Wow!" the lieutenant howled, as he slammed on his helmet and disappeared out the door. The pencil-pushing sergeant trailed him.

We were issued new rifles smeared with cosmoline and ordered to clean them. When I had finished mine, I had to record the serial number somewhere, so that I would always have it. In my wallet, I found a well-worn membership card to The Holy Name Society, which had been signed by an Amarillo chaplain. On the back of it I wrote, "Springfield 165558."

The rest of the day we heard a lecture on the nomenclature of the rifle. Everyone listened attentively. The room was silent except for the lecturing sergeant. He would tell us the complete story once, and once only; there was not time for more. If we missed something by dozing or not paying strict attention, it would be our lives that we were gambling. In the United States they were trained in a greater number of weeks than we would be trained in days. We had to absorb it all completely.

The sergeant finished the lecture with a very sober statement: "This is your rifle. Take the best care of it, for your very lives depend on it. It is the finest, most accurate army rifle in the world. It will not let you down if you take good care of it. You must know your rifle and know it thoroughly; know where it hits and how it hits. You will carry it through mud and dust; through rain and snow; hell and high water. You will sleep with it and pet it. Remember, it is your baby, so treat it with the best."

With the lecture soaking rapidly into me, I returned to our room, sat on the bed, and thought. No one really cared for me over here. There was no such thing as love. Every man lived for himself. We had to all stick together, but when it came to a real showdown, self-preservation was uppermost in every soldier's mind.

At that very moment I made up my mind to fight this war with all the skill and cunning I could master. I would never be taken prisoner. The captured soldiers that we had found with bullet holes in their heads and necks were too grim a reminder of a prisoner's fate. I would fight to the finish. I promised myself at this time so that in an hour of decision I would never have to stop and think what to do; my mind was already made up.

The days rolled slowly past, as we trained from the dark hours before dawn until long after the last glow of the setting sun had ebbed from the skies. Everyone drank it in with a serious mind. We were very earnest.

Each day we went to the firing range to study and fire one or more weapons. Each of us had to tear down and reassemble the weapon; then we fired it in teams, each taking his turn at the triggers of the rifle, mortar, carbine, and machine gun. When we had finished with the American weapons, the instructor gave us instructions and demonstrations with the enemy weapons. It would give each one an idea of the construction and sound of the things we would come upon in the near future.

The firing range was about three miles from the barracks. Each day, after clearing the damp, war-scarred town, we passed a racetrack and went on into a forest. As we crossed one of the many firebreaks I looked up at a sign attached to one of the larger trees. It stated that it was less than two kilometers to the sight of the signing of the armistice of 1918. An arrow pointed the direction.

Charley looked it over, "Doesn't mean anything now, does it?"

"Nope, it didn't amount to much," I added.

One evening, after consuming a considerable quantity of stew, my stomach began to grumble and gripe. Apparently this stew did not agree with me. I looked down at Charley rolling about on his bunk, occasionally giving off a light moan. Suddenly he jumped up. His green face was twisted with pain and with the speed of a racehorse he left the room.

Before long, I noticed that the others were having the same trouble.

By ten o'clock I had made five trips myself and was beginning to feel weak, but nearly cured. By that time I thought that I could go to sleep and rest until morning.

At three o'clock in the morning I was awakened with a start. I leaped from my bunk and raced out of the barracks, clad only in my long underclothing.

The latrine consisted of a long open trench about two hundred yards distant. The fresh snow glistened in the moonlight, and felt soft, but terribly cold, on my bare feet. I could see others dashing toward the trench from all directions. The entire camp must have been sick from the stew. Most of them were wearing the same attire as I, and many of them came forward with great speed, only to slow down to a walk a few yards from the trench; they didn't quite make it.

In the morning the training was confined to lectures, for no one, not even the instructors, felt well enough for bayonet practice or calisthenics. We went for a short walk to an open field on the river bank. There we crouched in the shelter of a straw stack and prepared to have a class in map reading. A blasted bridge and power plant lay before us.

A shrill whistle drew my attention to a hospital train making its way through the little village across the river. I remembered my ride on such a train. Now I was on the way back again—back to do it all over again. It reminded me of a criminal receiving an emergency operation so that he could live to be put to death in an electric chair.

Six days had passed since we had arrived, and our training was over. All that remained was the final examination consisting of one big night problem to determine how much of the training we had absorbed. It was different than the final examination we used to get in school. Here we would be graduated whether we passed or failed the examination.

The night problem was to be conducted in a forest a short distance away. As we left the camp grounds in a column of two's, we passed a large ordnance repair shop and got on the footpath which led to the forest. It was late afternoon, and the sunlight was fading.

To our left was a high rock wall, and at its foot, several crude wooden crosses marked the graves of a dozen or more enemy soldiers. One of them stood out above all the others, for it had been painted white. Black letters gave the name and rank of the German officer who rested beneath it. It made me turn my head in disgust. Why was he, even in death, so much better than the enlisted men who were killed with him? Why must his grave-marker be carved and painted while the others were merely weather-beaten boards nailed together?

As we slogged our way through the snow, slush, and mud, we sang a song picked up in England. It had a very enchanting melody and rhythm that went well with a soldier's pace.

A large pile of ammunition loomed up before us as we passed beneath the first trees of the forest. A soldier on guard walked slowly around it.

Our first task was to dig foxholes and camouflage them. Occasionally I could hear someone cussing a tree root giving him difficulty.

Shortly after dark the instructors came around and gave us the order of attack, issuing each of us two hand grenades and six rounds of ammunition for our rifles. The grenades contained sand. They would explode only strongly enough to sting the bare flesh. The slugs had been removed from the rifle shells and a wad of soap inserted. They would make a flash and noise, but would not work the automatic portion of the rifle.

Soon we were ordered to move up three hundred yards to the edge of a large, open field. We had to move quickly yet silently, for the enemy was supposed to be entrenched on the opposite side.

Suddenly the attack order was given, and we swept out over the field.

The rifles began to bang, and flashes could be seen over the entire area. A flare was shot into the air. Having been in combat before, I recognized it and dropped to the ground before it exploded in the air and illuminated the area.

When it exploded it gave me a chance to survey the field. Many soldiers continued to dash across the open space.

They did not know that it was wrong. It took much longer than a week to make a well-trained combat soldier.

The flare died, and once again I made my way across the field. A machine gun rattled. It had to be firing the real thing, for nothing less would make a machine gun work.

More flashes and grenades, then barbed wire entanglements, and the problem was over.

We assembled and returned to the barracks. Most were happy that the training was over, but I felt different. I was willing to train here for the duration of the war. As we cleaned our rifles and prepared for bed, the general topic of discussion was the problem that we had just finished. We all agreed that if we remedied the mistakes we had made that night things would go very well when the real test came.

The next morning we stood reveille and the roll was called by the lieutenant in charge of our barracks. He had received a battlefield commission in Africa. His salute was a rather odd display of military courtesy for a shot through the right hand during the early days of the invasion had made it nearly immovable.

After roll call he stood before us with his hands in

his pockets. His appearance was altogether different from the sharp little shavetails back in the United States.

"Now look, you birds," he started, "I came up the hard way, and I know what it's like to be an underdog combat man."

A rather silly grin appeared on his face as he continued, "This is Saturday morning, and there won't be another roll call until Monday night. You are to be shipped out Tuesday. Now that gives you three full days to get ready. I'm not allowed to authorize you to go anywhere, but maybe some of you can read between the lines. Just remember, if you get killed off this post, you will be termed AWOL, and your insurance is void. That's all. Dismissed!"

Over and above the gleeful roar of the happy soldiers I could hear the rough voice of the lieutenant—Lieutenant Kemkowski, "Now, damnit, don't you guys foul me up. I'm responsible, you know!"

After breakfast, Charley and I decided on a walk through the town. Most of the others had left without anything to eat, for many who had been stationed nearby were going back to visit their buddies or see a girl friend. As we cleared the gate, two of our roommates went rushing past.

"Where to?" I yelled after them.

"Rheims!" one said without looking back.

"Soissons!" the other shouted.

"What are you going to do there?" Charley asked.

"Women," they reported over their shoulders.

Leisurely we strolled down the cobblestone street. A long drive lined with flower beds and trees led to the right, so we followed it, for it seemed much more peaceful and beautiful than the street.

It led to the gate of the village cemetery, whose high rock walls were very forbidding. We peered between the steel bars of the huge gate, and saw tombstones, both large and small, littering the grounds. Many beautiful bouquets had been carefully placed on the various graves, making me think how seriously these people took death. I could still remember when it meant a great deal to me, but now it was no different from any of the other steps in the path of life.

Charley broke the silence, "I'll bet you can find dates in there a lot older than any in America."

I nodded my head in agreement. "Yes, I imagine this is an old cemetery."

"I'll bet I know how many are dead in there," said Charley, with a gesture.

"How did you figure that out?"

"That's easy," he laughed. "They're all dead."

We followed the path along the high wall in the general direction of the town. A fence of concrete posts and steel pipe took up where the high cemetery wall turned. When we looked out over the fence, a strange sight greeted our eyes. It was a French military cemetery of the last war.

Row upon row of crosses of graying concrete, blue-gray with moss, made it look similar to the cemeteries of our war dead.

We jumped the fence and wandered about. Small bouquets decorated some, while a few had pictures of fine young men in the uniform of the French army. Each cross had the name, rank, and the organization of the soldier beneath it. I observed that most were infantrymen, but a surprisingly large number were from the artillery, however. I wondered how that had happened. Perhaps they had been ambushed or maybe they had been killed in a last-ditch stand. I could well imagine that the people of this village knew what war was really like.

In the village we made our way through the crooked streets past heaps of rubble piled high on either side. One of the larger theaters had been taken over for American films to be shown to the American soldiers. A military policeman stood guard at the door.

Charley and I looked over the billboards and after finding that the movie suited us, we decided to take it in. Charley placed his hand on the handle to open the door.

"You can't go in there," barked the M. P.

"And why not?" demanded Charley.

"It's a full house."

"But we could sit on the floor."

"Nothing doing!"

Diplomatically, I approached him, "But, my good man," I pleaded, "we haven't seen a movie in a long time. Couldn't we just have a little peek?"

"Nope!" he shouted emphatically.

"How did you get your job?" I asked, trying to change the subject.

This started him off on a great speech. He told us that he had always done this—even in the U. S.

"Yep," he continued, "I used to especially like being on duty in front of the theater where the flying cadets get their wings. Used to get a dollar for each one I'd salute when they'd come out."

"How come?" I asked.

"Well, they are commissioned when they get their wings. It's the custom for an officer to pay a dollar to the first one to salute him, and I always tried to be that person. Used to clean up on that deal."

We left the theater, passed a large church, and entered a cafe. The beer was sweet and weak, and we sat and stared dreamily out the window at the passers-by.

A young woman, sitting at a table across the room, smiled at me, and I winked back as Charley watched the passing crowd.

The young lady finished her drink and came over. A large, black felt hat crowned her lovely figure. I offered her a chair as Charley's mouth dropped in amazement. He removed his helmet.

"Meet Camille," I told him.

"This is Charley," I said to her, pointing at my comrade.

After a short conversation we departed for her apartment. Charley was gleeful with thoughts of a wonderful time over the weekend.

"Two babes and two bottles of cognac," he whispered to me.

Once in the apartment we sprawled out on the sofa while Camille went into the next room to remove her wraps.

"Comfort," Charley groaned. "Solid comfort."

In a moment Camille reappeared. My eyes felt as if they would be pulled from their sockets; I could feel them bulging. Her fine figure and beautiful face were topped with a half-inch bristle of blonde hair. So that's why she wore such a large hat.

146

As she sat on the sofa between us I tried to be friendly, but I felt as if my real emotions were showing through. It made me uneasy as she explained the short hair to Charley. She did not need to explain to me; I knew.

At this time she could not get a job, for she had collaborated with the enemy. By shaving her head her countrymen had branded her so she could not rid herself of it for many months to come. Now, for a living, she could only sponge from the soft-hearted.

"What do you plan to do?" I asked her. "You can't go on like this."

"When my hair grows out, I'll go some place new and start all over again."

"And in the meantime?"

"Oh, I'll manage," she assured me. "A woman can always get by, especially where there are soldiers."

I could take it no longer.

"She's all yours," I told Charley as I headed for the door.

I walked down the street, across a large repaired bridge, and on to the railroad station to watch the traffic on the highway.

A truck stopped while the driver checked the oil and water in the motor.

"Going far?" I asked.

"Paris," came the reply. "Want a ride?"

A ride to Paris. It gave me a start.

"Yah, sure thing."

I jumped in and we roared off.

Paris was a great let-down to me, for it was not as beautiful and gay as I had expected. Perhaps I was in the wrong mood, or I may have been in the wrong section of the city for it was not bright and gay as I had pictured it.

Before long I noticed a white-helmeted military policeman following me. He was still half a block back, but his pace was almost deadly.

I had heard of others caught here without a pass. Nothing very severe happened, but they were arrested and held until a truckload accumulated going in the direction of their post. It sometimes took seven to ten days of waiting. I didn't want to foul up Lieutenant Kemkowski. This M. P. would never catch me; I wouldn't let him.

I increased my pace and went around a corner. Once out of sight of him, I ran fast until I thought it was about time for him to appear around the corner. When he came into view, I was walking, for if I were running, he might have been tempted to fire at me. I couldn't afford that.

Once again I looked back and saw that he had broken into a trot.

"Soldier!" he yelled, "Hey, soldier!"

Quickly I dashed into an open doorway and up the stairway. I opened the door at the head of the stairs and bolted into an apartment. I ran through the parlor, the kitchen, and out to the back porch. A middle-aged woman with a spatula in her hand yelled at me, but I paid no attention to her as I looked at the back yard below.

After dropping down the fire escape I ran across the yard and climbed two fences. This brought me to the alley. A brief run took me back to another street, where I found a hotel and ducked in.

My room was on the second floor. Here they called it the first floor for the one on the street level was called the ground floor.

I looked out the window and saw a jeep with two military policemen drive by on the street below. Kicking my shoes off, I decided to relax for awhile on the bed. Perhaps I could get out and move around after dark.

For dinner I got some black bread and soup in a near-by cafe. Even as I finished the soup, a jeep containing more military police passed on the street outside. I decided to go nowhere that night. The next day was Sunday. Perhaps they would be a bit more lax.

A grating, crashing noise jarred me from a deep sleep. I bounced to the edge of the bed as the lights were snapped on. The door had been smashed and lay flat on the floor well inside the room. Two men, dressed in civilian clothing, stood between the door and me. One sported an army automatic; the other held a sub-machine gun. They were both trained on me.

"Come on you dirty so and so," one growled in a perfect Southern drawl.

"Get on your feet and let's go," added the other.

I bent down to reach for my shoes.

"Oh, no, you don't!" yelled the one with the automatic, as he rushed toward me. "Get to your feet and don't try any tricks!"

I stood and started toward the door. The olive-drab long underwear was all the clothing I wore.

"Up on your toes and reach high," demanded the one carrying the machine gun.

I stretched my arms as much as I possibly could and walked high upon my toes.

We went down the stairway and out onto the sidewalk. The snow felt cold on my bare feet. A colored American soldier lay sprawled on the sidewalk. His fresh blood partially melted the snow and colored it a bright red. The body of a white soldier blocked the doorway to the cafe next door.

My two conquerors took me quickly to their headquarters, less than a block away. There I sat in a chair in the middle of the room, a bright light pouring down upon me.

Questions of my whereabouts during the last month were fired at me by half a dozen men. Most of them I could not see, for they stood in the ring of darkness on the outer edge of the room.

Before long they were satisfied that I was not a criminal, at least not the criminal they were searching for. The balance of clothing was tossed in a bundle at my feet, and the lights were turned on again in the room.

"Whew!" I sighed, as I began to put on my clothing. Then I asked them who they were and what they were after.

They explained to me that they were members of the Criminal Investigation Department, something on the order of an army FBI. They were cracking down on a group of deserters who were operating a large-scale black market ring in gasoline, cigarettes, and other American supplies. These criminals had gone so far as to have a setup to remove the color from the gasoline so that it could not be recognized as that of the army.

It just so happened that I had obtained a hotel room between the two rooms where the black marketeers had been staying during the past week. A soldier and a French girl had been taken from the one just a few minutes before I was taken. Two others tried to shoot it out in the cafe below; it was their bodies that we had passed on the way over.

When I had finished dressing, one of them handed me my wallet. "Well, you can go back to your room and sleep," he said.

"Are you kidding?" I asked, as I grinned at him. "Hell, I won't sleep for a week after this."

I returned to the hotel room, propped the broken door over the opening, and went to bed. Sleep was impossible, for I could see nothing but the muzzle of an army forty-five. It seemed large enough to crawl into.

Early Sunday morning I slipped through the streets and got back onto the highway leading to camp.

Getting back was much more difficult than the trip down, for it took many short rides with long walks in between. A cold wind cut at my face and hands and passed through my several thicknesses of woolen clothing.

At five-thirty Monday afternoon all of us, with the exception of three, stood in formation for retreat in an open drill field just outside the camp walls. We stood at attention while a band played both the American and French national anthems. A large group of poorly clad civilians stood with bared and bowed heads at one end of the field, watching in silence as the flags of both countries were brought down and folded.

After retreat we were to be fed a chicken dinner. The menu read chicken, but we were fed hash. Everyone grumbled in disgust.

"The brass must be having a banquet with some French babes," snorted Charley.

After dinner we completed our packing while everyone exchanged addresses. I got out the small black address book that had been with me for over a year and contained the names and addresses of people all over the world. As I thumbed through it, I recalled the wonderful experiences of the past.

There was Shirley, of Longview, Texas, a wonderful telephone operator, with whom I had shared many an enjoyable Sunday. I remembered the week-day evenings when time was short. Instead of my going to her home to get her, we would meet beneath the big clock on the main street and start out from there.

I paged through the book. Several soldiers addresses had the word "deceased" written over them. Yes, they were my friends, my schoolmates, and my buddies. They were the fellows who had graduated from high school in the classes from 1937 to 1940. Most of them had served in the army for two or three years. Take George Lally, for instance, who was graduated with the class of thirty-nine, and after spending two years in college, had entered the service. In the first part of forty-two he finished bombardier school and was killed in October of forty-three when his plane was shot down during the bombing of the ball-bearing factories in Schweinfurt.

Charley sat silently on his bunk below.

"Have any girl friends?" I asked.

"Yes, or at least I used to," he answered, rather weakly. "She's been getting pretty high and mighty lately. The last two letters have been very sour."

He handed me three pictures. One of them was of his parents standing before their lovely home. The other two were of Charley and a cute brunette. They had their arms about each other's waist. He wore a summer uniform; she, a beautiful flowered dress, while the same fine home comprised the background.

"What seems to be the trouble?" I asked.

"I'm not sure," he replied, "but I think she has found someone else."

"How long has it been since you last saw her?"

"Little over two years."

I handed back his pictures and went about getting the names and addresses of the others in the room.

One fellow, named Pflueger, told me that it wouldn't do any good to take his name and address, for he was sure he would be dead before Christmas. He looked down at his feet, then added wryly, "They can't change this first-class engineer into a first-class infantryman so quick. You know, I'm not worth a damn at anything that's second rate with me."

Early the next morning we were fed and then assembled in a large building. A captain from an armored division gave us some last minute advice, telling us to fight with everything available, that we must sharpen our senses to a higher pitch than we ever knew possible. In close combat we should fight like wildcats.

"And in finishing," his sharp voice crackled in the

room, "I want to warn you not to call a combat medic a pillroller. If you do, you'll eat it a hundred times over. They're the only ones around that can patch up the leaking holes that the krauts shoot into your carcass."

"By the way," he added, "I believe we have a combat medic in our midst. I wonder if we can get him to stand up?"

I thought that perhaps he was talking of me, but I was not sure. I decided to remain seated and wait.

He turned to the sergeant beside him and asked the name. The sergeant told him, and he called my name out loudly.

Slowly, I rose to my feet. It made me feel flustered and rather foolish.

"Sure! There he is," shouted the captain. "That's one of the Moselle River Rats. He's been through the mill. Knows what it's like to stare the enemy in the eye. He felt the sting of the enemy too."

The captain finished. As I sat down my face felt hot enough to be on fire.

The lecture ended, and we left the building. As we filed through the doorway we were handed one day's supply of K rations.

Once again we climbed aboard a convoy of six by sixes, sixteen to a truck. We were about to cover another lap on the way to the front.

It wouldn't be long now. Most of us would be in action by the end of this week, and without a doubt some would never see the beginning of another.

VII.

WE arrived in Verviers, Belgium, and made our quarters in an automotive repair garage.

After unrolling my sleeping bag on the hardwood floor I walked over to look at the automobiles stored in one corner of the building. The Opel, which appeared very small in comparison to the American automobiles, seemed to be in the majority.

"Imagine going a hundred and twenty miles an hour in that," interrupted a voice beside me.

It was Charley who was interested also.

"But that's kilometers," I told him. "That would only be about seventy-five miles an hour."

A civilian approached. "Very good," he stated, patting the fender of the Opel.

"Belgique?" I asked.

"No! Boche!" he snorted.

I went on to ask him if it belonged to him and how long it had been there. He replied that it belonged to another citizen of the town and that it had been here for many months.

"Nix benzine!" he shouted as he raised his hands in a gesture to show that there was nothing he nor anyone else could do about it.

"What's he say?" asked Charley.

"Oh, that it's a German made car owned by a Belgian. It's a good car, but they can't run it because there is no gasoline."

"It sounded to me like he was speaking French."

"Oh, sure. All the Belgians around here do," I told him.

"Live and learn," he muttered as we headed for the outside.

The first place we went for was the latrine in a building across the street. It consisted of several stalls, but instead of the usual closet bowl it had two upraised treads upon which to place one's feet, and a four-inch hole in between. It was made of fine tile.

As we left the building, Charley remarked, "Why must they do everything the hard way over here?"

Hardly had we gone a block when a putt-putt noise brought us to a halt. It came from a far distance, and at first sounded north, then east. We could not tell its exact location.

Suddenly it stopped. The entire buzzing of the city had stopped also as a deadly silence reigned over the area. The few remaining soldiers and civilians still in the streets were down on their elbows and knees. They held their heads down with their eyes closed tightly and their mouths opened wide. They waited in fear of the sudden horrible death brought about by concussion.

Charley and I each sensed the danger and quickly ducked down.

The long seconds passed slowly as we waited in silence, while intense fear clutched at my very heart. Waiting for something unknown was a feeling which I had experienced before, a long time before.

When it hit, it gave my body the same working over that it had experienced before the break-through in Normandy—the working over brought about by our heavy bombers. It felt as if I were being squeezed so hard that my tongue would be shot from my mouth like a bullet.

We waited for a moment after the explosion and, seeing the others in the street get up, we did likewise.

"What in the world is that?" asked Charley.

"I'm not sure," I told him, "but from what I've heard through the grapevine I think it's a buzz bomb."

"You mean the V-1 rocket?"

"Yep."

"That's what was coming into England when I was there. Of course, none landed in our area."

"How come they get on their knees and elbows?" I asked.

"Well, from what they tell me," Charley went on to explain, "you must allow some of the blast to pass under as well as over you. If the bomb lands too close, it may smash you right into the street, unless part of the explosion is allowed to pass beneath you."

We went back to our quarters, grabbed our mess kits, and headed for the mess hall in a factory building about two blocks away.

When we had finished eating, we had to go out in the street to wash our mess kits. As we passed through the door, a dozen hungry faces stared up at us—faces of all ages and descriptions. They begged for the last few drops of coffee left in a cup or a dried-up sausage skin about to be thrown from a mess kit. A bit of gravy remained in mine, so an elderly woman wiped it clean with her finger. I smiled down upon her as she thanked me and bowed from the waist.

As I walked toward the boiling tubs of water, I looked back and saw that she was still licking her fingers and smacking her lips. It was then that I realized that I could never stay here. I could watch well-fed young men shoot one another to bits. But never could I, a well-fed soldier, have stood by and watched innocent people slowly starve to death. My heart was hard and cold, but in a different manner. I could not look upon the little, homeless children, clothed in rags, with sunken eyes and swollen bellies. Their longing look pierced me through and through.

There was a shower location six blocks down the street where we were allowed to go in small groups. When we had finished taking our showers, we were given a complete issue of clean socks and underclothing. They were not new, but had been freshly laundered. It made us feel refreshed.

Instead of going directly back to our quarters I decided to walk about the town. As I wandered down the narrow winding streets I could see how empty the stores were. These poor people, living in a ravished land, had been beaten into submission and then robbed of everything that was valuable.

Occasionally a door with "Off Limits," written in dripping paint, showed up. They were houses of prostitution, which were bad medicine for American soldiers. Some took it seriously, while others remarked that it just made it easier for them to find. Anyone caught there, however, was sent to a medical station for examination and observation.

In the window of one of the larger fish markets sat a barrel of Rollmops. As I stood there and gazed at it, the saliva began to flow freely in my mouth, for it had been ever so long since I had had any—perhaps three or four years. I only knew that I would not be able to sleep that night unless I had some. Never before had I ever experienced such a strong desire for any food.

As I entered the market I could see the face of the proprietor light up. He was overjoyed to see me come in, and taking my arm led me behind the counter and offered me a chair. I refused to sit, and told him that I would like some of the Rollmops. I then proceeded to explain that I had no ration card but would pay him well.

Taking two from the barrel, he placed them on a piece of paper on the counter. As I picked one up to eat it, he noticed the scar of the bullet wound on my right hand.

"Boche?" he asked, pointing to it.

I nodded my head and presented the other hand. He took it in his hands and examined it closely, turning it over and back again.

"Here?" he asked, pointing toward the floor in a manner to show me that he meant in Belgium.

"No. *La France*," I answered, pointing to the south.

He nodded his head to show that he understood and then shook it to show that he didn't like it. He darted for the back room, and, upon returning, had a straight pin in one hand and a small piece of ribbon in the other. The ribbon was of the colors of Belgium—black, yellow, and red. With great pride he pinned it to the breast of my field jacket.

Then he went on to explain that the people of this city pinned one of these on each of the first group of combat men to enter the city. They were happy for the first time in four years—the enemy had been driven out. They were free again.

He pinned this ribbon on me because I had fought and bled in the liberation of a friendly, neighboring country.

I climbed a steep hill by a series of stairways and winding footpaths. Most of the houses on the hillside were surrounded by great stone walls covered with a heavy climbing vine, while wire fences closed in the small vineyards spotting the area.

Once at the top, I sat down to rest. The tile roofs of the city below presented a picture like those I remembered from my grade-school reader. The city lay in a large bowl-shaped valley. It was on the rim of this bowl that the greater number of buzz bombs had been landing. Occasionally one skimmed over and landed in the heart of the city.

After spending an hour or so gazing at the struggling scene below, I descended and headed in the direction of our quarters.

Suddenly it came again. I could hear the motor of another buzz bomb causing the air to throb and thump. I scanned the skies to see if I could locate it, but it was nowhere to be seen. When the motor stopped, it seemed to be directly overhead, so I got down on my knees and elbows to wait. I could feel the perspiration break out on my forehead and upper lip. It caused my skin to itch.

A buzz bomb was one of the most unpredictable weapons. It did not follow any set pattern of flight, and there was nothing one could do or a place one could go to be safe from it. When the motor stopped, some of them went into a straight glide, others made a horseshoe turn and descended, while still others plunged almost straight down. One night I watched several in the dark, and I could see the light from the explosions which propelled them. I saw where they shut off and then watched to see where they would land. Most of them landed on the ridge surrounding the city.

After a moment or so of waiting, a terrific explosion rocked the very foundation of the area. It must have been quite close for I could feel the air rush over me. From all indications, it must have hit very close to our quarters, so I jumped up and ran in that direction.

When I got there, I found that it had landed in a huge gas supply tank used to supply the city. For a radius of three blocks dead soldiers and civilians littered the streets. Those farthest from it seemed to have just lain down for a nap, for they lay with a peaceful look upon their tired faces. There was not a hair out of place or a bruise upon their bodies.

A greater number lay about near the ruptured gas tank. The bodies had been blown and thrown in a disorderly fashion; the stomachs had been split wide open and the intestines exposed. The shoes of others had popped their seams and were scattered about, while the eyeballs of most were out of their sockets.

The huge tank reminded me of a giant tin can that had been burst by a fire cracker. Not a window was intact as far as I could see. The brick walls of the surrounding buildings were scorched black and brown. One of them was our mess hall.

I glanced into a sidewalk latrine and saw two American soldiers slumped on the concrete floor. Undoubtedly they had not known that the bomb was approaching. I walked over to the body of a ten or twelve year old girl, as she lay face-down in the gutter. Kneeling beside her, I gently rolled her over. The eyeballs came to rest upon her cheeks; her mouth opened wide. She seemed to have swallowed her tongue, for it was turned up and jammed down her throat—like the work of some fiend. In her waxy hand she still gripped a small, white handkerchief. My heart seemed about to explode as I looked upon the bluing face.

I could feel water running down my cheeks. Quickly I wiped it away, and jumping up, walked away as big and unconcerned as I could possibly pretend.

As I entered our quarters an elderly man pressed a piece of paper into my hand. Quickly I opened it and read, "Try the house of Madame Toubais." It went on to give the address, but I did not read it. I looked for the old man, but he was gone. Such tripe. With anger I ripped up the paper and tossed it into the wind.

Trucks took us to the next station, which consisted merely of a tent, through which we passed in rapid succession. A lone soldier broke open the cases of rifle ammunition and gave each of us five bandoleers—one to fill the cartridge belt and the others to be put about our necks.

It was here that we were assigned to a division. Trucks picked us up to take us to our respective organizations.

When we had traveled only a short distance, a sign let us know that we were no longer in Belgium. It read, "You are entering an enemy country—be alert."

The white dragon's teeth of the enemy's defense made me understand that the enemy land was well fortified. Here there would be no freedom-loving people to help us; everyone was an enemy. We would fight everyone and everything, especially the weather.

At battalion headquarters we were checked in and fed. We were to go to our companies at night under the cover of darkness.

As I looked about the little *dorf* in which the battalion headquarters was located, I could see that we were unwanted guests of the German people. They did not smile as the French and Belgian people did; they met us with looks of hate and defiance. Here every soldier walked about with a loaded rifle with instructions to shoot, without hesitation, anyone who tried to start a disturbance.

In France, I had witnessed the hanging of an American soldier for harming a French girl. He was given a trial, found guilty, and hanged in the public square of the village in which he had done his misdeed.

Here it was altogether a different proposition. We could take whatever we wanted, in any manner we saw fit. No one would take action against us, for we were the conquerors in the back yard of the enemy. He had to bow to our every wish.

The snow began to fall as we started to trudge toward the company. The wind caused it to drift and whip up into our faces. I was thankful for the scarf that had been given to me in Belgium for it went up and over my head, as well as about my neck. It was warmer than being without one, but still the wind cut through it.

About midnight we were taken into a battered building to meet a bearded captain. He introduced himself as Captain Slye and assigned me to fill a vacancy in the first squad of the first platoon; I was to be the first scout.

"You can have the honor of being the first American soldier to enter a lot of these German towns," he advised me.

I gulped. Me a first scout with the small amount of training that I had had? Oh, well, I'd keep my eyes open and hope that we wouldn't run into anything too stiff for a day or so until I got a bit used to things.

"Go into that room," he ordered, pointing to a door. "Make yourself as comfortable as you can for the night."

Leaving the door open so that I could see, I unrolled the sleeping bag on the floor. I could see several men lying about on the floor, most of whom slept with their helmets on. All were fully clothed, and a loaded weapon of some type rested with each of them.

Hardly had I stretched out when a voice called out, "All scouts—let's go!"

I grabbed my rifle and went into the other room. A lieutenant and half a dozen others were already preparing to go someplace. Without question I joined the little circle for instructions.

We were going to blow up a pillbox. "Pillbox A" or "P.B.A.," the lieutenant called it. My instructions were to lead the way and, with the help of another scout, to blow it open.

164

As we trudged off through the dark, blizzard-howling night, I began thinking to myself, "This is only a practice mission. Certainly they wouldn't pick me, an inexperienced scout, to lead the way if this were the real thing. No, the army doesn't do things that way. They have always taken good care of me before, and certainly this is no different. Besides, if this were the real thing, they would want to make sure that it went right—they would choose an experienced man. Yes, of course, this is only a make-believe setup to allow us to become familiar with what we will be confronted with later on."

We halted in the fluffy, knee-deep snow. The blizzard swirled about as the lieutenant came up from the rear. Taking two of us by the arm, he spoke to us in a low monotone.

"Frank," said he, "you and Hildebrand set this pole charge off against the door. Do it as quickly and quietly as possible. Stay there to make sure it goes off right."

We nodded.

The pillbox was well situated in the side of a small hill, so with considerable caution we moved in on it. I was thankful for the cold and snow, for it protected us from the mines which must have been planted as thickly as wheat.

Hildebrand lit the fuse and I nudged the long stick against the steel door. We watched it for a second, and then rolled over a couple of times to get behind a small mound. I pressed my face into the snow, opened my mouth wide, and threw my arms up over my head and face.

The explosion ripped open the door. In a split second

two riflemen dashed through it and stood, alert, in the concrete corridor inside. Quickly, Hildebrand and I followed them in the same manner.

There were two steel doors on each side of the corridor.

"If anyone sticks a head out, blow it off!" shouted the lieutenant.

While we stood there on guard, the others busied themselves unloading the heavy satchels from their backs and stacking them in a large pile in the corridor. Each satchel contained many small bricks of high explosive.

The lieutenant prepared a fuse while another soldier argued with him that it was not long enough.

"But we don't want those birds to come out and yank it out," declared the lieutenant.

"Okay," sighed the other in dismay.

We were ordered to leave. As we passed through the doorway, the lieutenant lit the fuse. We ran like frightened rabbits.

I thrashed through the snow with great effort, but when I saw the flash from the explosion I dived to the ground.

It seemed ages before everything stopped falling. I got up on my knees, my rifle in hand, and turned to face the pillbox. There was not a sound. Nothing moved. The pillbox was but a gaping hole in the earth. Slowly, others rose out of the snow around me. Then we assembled.

The lieutenant was missing. We fanned out to look for him, for he must be found before the enemy began shelling.

I came across half a body lying in the snow. It was not the lieutenant; it was a German. It even smelled of German tobacco.

"Here he is!" sounded a voice.

We all converged on the spot.

"Dead," we each muttered to ourself.

A huge boulder of concrete had fallen upon him, crushing him to death. Hildebrand and I picked up the limp, still warm body and carried it back to the C.P. There Captain Slye looked it over and told us to put it in the garage just around the corner.

We placed him on the floor of the garage beside several others. Hildebrand folded his hands upon his breast and closed the door. We returned to our room to try for a bit more sleep.

Sleep was difficult. Over and over again I reenacted the mission in my mind. Yes, I had been baptized under fire before, but what a way to be initiated into the infantry.

This continued without end, day after day, night after night. P.B.-X; P.B.-Y. There were always half a dozen more hidden about us. Even the coast defense was not this deep.

Sometimes they proved too much for frontal assault, so Hildebrand and I crawled around to the rear, while the others kept the enemy busy from the front. While sprawled out on top, I cautiously lowered a horseshoe-shaped explosive by means of a wire until it rested upon the barrel of a protruding weapon. Upon exploding it put the weapon out of commission.

It was very effective, but extremely dangerous, for the margin by which the explosion passed over one's head was very narrow. One of the greatest dangers, however, was the possibility of being seen and fired upon by another pillbox, for they were arranged to protect one another in cases such as this.

As time went on, I managed to secure a pair of painter's white coveralls for camouflage purposes. From the medic, I got adhesive tape to wrap about my rifle in various places to break its outline. A piece of sheet took care of my helmet.

The rest of the company got camouflaged with the aid of sheets, pillowcases, tablecloths, and other white materials. It worked well, but it was very obvious that they were not tailor-made.

I went over beside Charley. He was struggling with a white skirt, trying to make it easier for his legs to move.

"Damn!" he grunted. "I read a while back where all the combat troops were to have snow capes by now. I guess the rear echelon Air Corps and Quartermaster don't have their fill yet, though."

I chuckled quite loudly. He stopped fixing the skirt and raised up, his face as red as a pickled beet. He was mad enough to explode.

"It's the truth," he spat. "Just like it was with combat boots. Hell, every ward boy and finance pencil-pusher had them, even when we were back there. Look at your buddies here. Over half still have leggings."

In the meantime, another scout, an Oklahoma Indian, came up and listened with intent interest but said nothing. His face was expressionless. He was a true infantryman—could fight anything to a finish. I liked to have him along on patrol.

"Well, what do you think, Chief?" I asked.

"He's right," he stated, pointing at Charley. "But I bet the people and congress in America don't know about it. I think they mean well."

"Yah, but what can you do about it?" snorted Charley.

Chief walked away.

"Maybe we should write to the Great White Father in Washington," he replied over his shoulder.

That brought a smile, even from Charley.

We battled our way to the edge of the great Hurtgen Forest, which looked ever dark and forbidding. Here, we, the shivering infantry, dug in. There were no buildings for shelter and no fires to drive the chill from our freezing torsos.

Each day we drove only a few yards. The enemy lurked behind every clump and tree trunk and forced us to crawl all the way. He who stood was hit by a dozen bullets.

The tree bursts were deadly, for there was no protection from them. When a mortar or artillery shell hit a treetop, it scattered red-hot shrapnel over a fifty-yard area. Even the holes that were covered with logs were not complete protection. After each explosion the dying and wounded could be heard.

It was mid-morning before daylight came into the forest; it left by mid-afternoon. The long nights brought a bit more activity than could be observed during the daytime.

Each night the first four men of my squad went on a patrol of some type. Being the first scout, I usually led the little band. Hildebrand, a short, dark-complexioned fellow from Kansas, stuck close to me. Several times he saved my life by routing or killing an enemy soldier who was bringing an aim on me. Each time I thanked him, he told me, "I'm only thankful that I'm not in your place. You see, they are hid and don't move until you go by. They must move to prepare to shoot. That's when I see them."

"I'm still mighty thankful," I insisted.

His black, beady eyes twinkled beneath their bushy brows.

"I hope I see them all," he added.

Brinker, an Indiana college student, followed Hildebrand. He was the rifle grenadier of the squad; therefore, his rifle had a special fixture to fire antitank grenades. His clothing hung upon his sad physique in a very ungainly manner. His strength lay in his brain. Often I referred to him as the inverted Atlas type— wide hips and narrow, slanting shoulders. He laughed each time, a cigarette usually hanging from his lower lip.

Then there was Boblo, a freckle-faced New Englander yet in his teens. From his actions one would think that he had not yet had a serious thought in his mind. He was a true infantryman, armed to the teeth with pistols and trenchknives, and somewhere along the line had found a second belt of magazines for his BAR. He carried a couple of extra bandoleers of ammunition, also.

He did not have the beard that the rest of us had, so I took particular notice of his well-formed teeth. They were turning a dingy yellow from the lack of care.

It bothered me, so I asked him why he didn't brush them a bit.

"Well, it's like this," he said, preparing for quite a speech. "I used to take awful good care of them. When I came up here, they gave me some of that damn Limey toothpowder in a paper tube. You know the stuff I mean. Well, right off the bat it got damp and hardened up; then it froze up. I got mad one morning and threw the whole business out—toothbrush and all."

I thought for a moment. Yes, I knew the worthless tooth powder to which he referred—nothing more than baking soda. It was too bad they didn't issue a small quantity of good tooth cleanser in every breakfast ration, for it would have been better than the cigarettes, which several of us did not smoke.

"You can get by with just a toothbrush," I advised him. "It does a good job, even if it doesn't always taste so well."

I pulled mine out of my shirt pocket to show him.

"It has a bit of lint and dirt on it," I laughed, "but what's a little dirt among dirty friends?"

"Okay," he said, "I'll see if I can pick one up. But I'm not taking one off any of these stiffs."

Fighting in the cold winter was much different from that of the warmer days. The clothing we were forced to wear made moving quickly a near impossibility. At this time the cold was very severe, making the snow squeak under our feet. I put a fold of my scarf up over my mouth and nose, only to have the frost collect on it rather than on my beard.

For the past few days I had been considering the task of shaving. Hildebrand and I shared the same foxhole, but each time I mentioned a fire to heat some water he disagreed.

"It would take too much of a fire," he told me. "First of all, you must melt the snow, and then you must get the water hot. A fire like that would make too much smoke in the daytime and too much light at night."

I agreed with him. Brinker could have told us the exact number of calories it would have taken to do the job. He was intelligent, so I decided to get some of his ideas on the subject.

He and Boblo were in a hole a few yards away. To have talked to him that day was an impossibility for during the past few days no one had been able to put his head above the ground level without drawing half a dozen shots. The enemy was numerous and only a short distance away. Even going to the latrine had become a problem, so we solved it by using a ration box and throwing it away. We lost what little modesty we had left.

I watched Hildebrand prepare his supper ration. In making the lemonade from the powder in his ration, he heated a bit of water from his canteen by using the wax-coated inner box of the rations. With care, he cut a small hole in a side, near the bottom, to give the necessary draft to keep it burning. Placing it on the ground, he lit the open end.

"Lemonade and grapefruit," he grumbled. "That's all I've ever had since I got into the army. It's enough to eat the lining out of a leather boot. I'll bet some senator must have a citrus ranch in the states."

I thought that two of these boxes would be sufficient to melt the snow, but there were none to be had.

Then I remembered that we had been issued a small pocket stove back in France. They were of German make—apparently captured in an army supply dump. I had to search through my pockets, for I hadn't seen it since it was issued to me. When I produced it, Hildebrand wanted to know what it was.

"Oh, our army has something like that," he told me. "Only it isn't in a metal case as that one is."

I looked it over and read some of the things stamped into it: "*Kocher, Mod. 9; hier aufklappen.*" It had pictured instructions so that even the illiterate could understand it.

I opened it and removed the large, frosty-looking chemical brick inside. After breaking off a section of it, I read what was printed in the bottom of the metal container: "*Tablettenauflage.*" Then it went on to give the manufacturer's name and address.

"So it was made in Stuttgart-W?" I grumbled. "I'll bet the women and old men that helped make this never dreamed that some American dogface would be using it."

"No," volunteered Hildebrand. "I'll bet they had visions of some German hero, with a clean uniform and Iron Cross, using it in a neat shelter. Or maybe in a cool woodland, after a hot day, the beautiful sunset as a background."

"Stop it!" I yelled. "You're driving me nuts!"

I placed a canteen cup of snow on the little cooker and waited for it to get warm. With Hildebrand's bar of soap and my razor I managed to yank the beard from my face. I rinsed the balance of the lather by dipping my finger into the water and wiping it off. It dried almost immediately.

Hildebrand still sipped his lemonade. He stared.

"Why so mum?" I asked.

"Just thinking. No wonder the army's so sour. I, alone, have consumed more lemonade already than any four Americans do in a lifetime."

We laughed it off.

The morale at the front was wonderful. We knew that we didn't have a job with a lot of class, but someone had to do it. What we would have liked to have seen, however, was an occasional change-about, perhaps some work in the rear area while others met the enemy. It would have been better all around. To show our appreciation for a rear area job, we would have done it the most efficient way. It would have given some of the rear echelon grumblers a chance to have proven that they would rather have been in combat, or at least made them appreciate living.

Boblo got his say in, "It would give them a chance to get first crack at some of this 'women and wine' that we are supposed to get."

"Yah, the Air Corps can look forward to a trip home," said Brinker. "All they have to do is complete so many missions. What do we have to look forward to? They stick us here and here we stay until we are either burned out or shot to hell."

"What are you grumbling about?" yelled Hildebrand. "You know what they tell the Germans when they gripe, don't you?"

"No, what?" I asked.

Dramatically, he bowed his head and pointed his

finger like a stern father sending his boy off to bed without supper, "Back! Back to the Russian front!"

A shell sent us scurrying. Our artillery opened up; it was barely clearing us. Those howitzers were wonderful; so were the teams that operated them. Time and again we had taken dazed prisoners who asked us to show them the new type of machine gun artillery piece that we had. It came in so fast and so accurately that it knocked the skids out from under anyone. The prisoners told us that they had never been hit so hard and so fast before; it just rained upon a small area. These prisoners were through. They did not resist, but were sorry that they had ever heard of war.

When we told them it was just regular artillery batteries, they did not believe us. "Just can't be," they said. The Germans were the master race. No one could outdo them, especially these soft Americans, their dictator had told them. If there were better artillery batteries to be had, they would have had them.

In between shells we could hear Boblo singing his favorite artillery song:

"Here's one high; there's one low.
Where the hell did that one go?
As those drunkards keep throwing them in."

The solemn solitude of a night in a heavy forest was awe-inspiring. There was no movement of air and sparkling frost lay upon the clean, fluffy, new-fallen snow. A break in the heavens exposed the shimmering stars and a bright silvery moon. An occasional hare could be seen playing and skipping about in the distance. I felt alone; all alone. As I looked out over the shadows of the towering pines, it made me want to sleep and dream. I wanted to throw a kiss to the moon and crawl into a soft, warm bed for a long night of sleep.

A sudden realization brought me back. I huddled, shivering in the frozen hole, a single blanket wrapped about me. I had long since thrown away the sleeping bag, for safety's sake. The rifle stuck up between my half-bent knees. My mother would never have stood for this—out in the open with one blanket in sub-zero temperatures. I could hear her scolding, "My goodness, boy! Get more blankets! You'll catch your death of cold!"

The lemonade that we made during the past few days from the water in our canteen had a peculiar tingle. Each morning Doc came around to put a shot of medical alcohol into the canteens. It was hard on the lining of one's stomach, but it prevented the water from freezing. Some of the fellows would have liked an overdose to make them feel high, but it was an impossibility; one would have gotten sick first. Even bouillon powder could not disguise its bitterness.

Each night Hildebrand and I left the safety of our hole to go on a detail of some type. Occasionally it was an observation patrol into enemy territory, but most of the time it was a plain detail. Sometimes we planted mines or strung barbed wire.

The most undesirable was the stiff detail. It consisted of collecting the frozen bodies of the dead from no man's land. For this I liked to have Boblo as a partner, for he took some of the soberness from the job.

We took them back several hundred yards and

stacked them in a shed. Every other day we stayed there long enough to load them into a truck for transport back to a cemetery.

We tossed the frozen bodies up over the racks. The first few boomed loudly on the steel bottom, but after a short time the bottom was covered, and they landed with a dull thud. The enemy soldiers were loaded first; then the Americans were piled on top. Usually there was a good truckload.

Once again we tried to push on. The resistance was stiff—nearly overwhelmingly stiff. We crawled, rolled, ducked, and dodged. Small glass and plastic mines shattered the feet of many, for glass and plastic could not be indicated by the detector. The deadly schu-mine took its toll. Barbed wire and fallen treetops added to the confusion.

At times it seemed as if we would be overrun. We were seasoned veterans at forest fighting now; we were sly and made good use of every opportunity. Our rifles would shoot through any tree in the forest and still have power enough to kill a man. Most recruits did not know this and would not fire at a man hiding behind a tree trunk. We no longer threw the hand grenades wildly, but with care and precision; they exploded two or three feet from the ground. Brinker once figured that when they were thrown in this manner, each should kill or wound three of the enemy, if they were scattered in the usual manner. He counted off the forty-eight squares into which the grenade was molded, then figured it into some equation.

The machine gun rattled; it made music in our ears. Brinker fired an anti-tank grenade at an enemy hasty-fortification. It was shattered to pieces in a cloud of white smoke.

The enemy was using more automatic weapons than usual. The machine-pistols burped fast and furious, sounding like canvas being torn. The bark flew from the trees before them. We crouched low, ever so low.

Throughout the day we fought with all the strength we could muster, but still it went much like a football game. First we gained two hundred yards, then were thrown back. Each time we wiggled our way back toward the newly lost ground, we were met by more fire from the enemy weapons, mines, and booby traps.

I saw our aid man bandage the hand of a wounded comrade. As they knelt in the snow, facing one another, a large caliber bullet severed the wounded hand from the outstretched arm. The medic stared at the hand, still hanging in the untied bandages. The other soldier gaped at the squirting stump.

A short time later the aid man was killed in no man's land. He had crawled out to give aid to a soldier who had been wounded and left the last time we had advanced that far. In our absence the enemy had booby-trapped the unconscious man. As the aid man tried to help him a blast ripped both to shreds.

As night closed in about us once again, we fell, exhausted, into the same holes we had occupied the night before. We had gained nothing, not an inch of soil. We had lost some very brave men and most of our ammunition. That night our ammunition could be replaced.

When the sweat of the day evaporated from our bodies we began to feel the chill of the oncoming night. The scarfs were wrapped about our heads, collars were buttoned, and the remaining blankets drooped over bent shoulders. We prepared to shiver through another night.

Even before the heavy breathing subsided, the scouts were called out to string barbed wire and plant mines.

VIII.

A<small>N</small> overcoat was a thing of the past for the infantry because they had been left in England. Only the enemy wore an ankle-long covering of warmth. At times we envied them but knowingly understood that safety demanded that we wear only a field jacket.

We depended upon the finely woven woolen clothing to keep us from freezing—one suit of long underwear and two issues of woolen shirts and pants. They were not as loose and bulky as those of other armies. We, whose life depended upon speed and agility, really appreciated this superior grade of clothing.

Propaganda broadcasts had been increasing lately. A woman played records of well-known American songs and between each record urged us to surrender and to make ourselves available to the fine German prisoner-of-war camps. There we would be safe and could wait in peace until the war was won by them. There we would be spared the horrors yet to come and would be kept well fed and warm. Most of us laughed it off. Others worried us by taking it a bit seriously.

Several shells containing leaflet propaganda had landed among us. One leaflet showed an American soldier trying to dig a foxhole through the snow while a blizzard swirled about him. A cloaked skeleton with a sickle hovered overhead. Across the bottom, in bold type, was written, "Your first winter in Europe."

Another showed the picture of a lovely wife stating a few so-called facts: "This is the way the future is made . . ." It was sponsored by the "POW Life Assurance Co., with no premiums to pay." It stated that the average GI Joe in combat reached the age of 23.2 years. The average age of the American at the time of death was 60.5 years. Therefore POW's lived longer by 37.3 years.

Still another showed a middle-aged woman kneeling before a cross in a military cemetery. The caption read: "Congress has voted a law entitling Gold Star Mothers to a free trip to Europe after the war. Is this to be your mother?"

Some had the pictures of a 4F sitting in a cafe. A scantily dressed girl sat on each knee, feeding him a cocktail. It stated: "Your wives and sweethearts are doing their part."

A few of them tried another angle. They showed fine photographs of a little girl with a disappointed look upon her face. She asked, "Daddy, why didn't you come home for Xmas?"

On a cold, foggy, December morning the Germans started off by opening up with a thundering artillery barrage. Dozens of infantrymen swarmed toward us. They fell like flies before our murderous fire, for everyone was raking the area—everyone but Boblo. As I looked over toward his foxhole I could see that he was working feverishly with his automatic rifle. Apparently it had jammed.

I crawled over to his hole, thinking that perhaps the two of us together could make it work. Brinker was sprawled out behind a log beside the foxhole. As I examined the stalled weapon, I could see him out of the corner of my eye, ducking and dodging between shots.

A quick examination proved that the rifle had been frozen solid. Something had to be done and done quickly, for we had to have the firepower of this automatic weapon to hold the onrush of the enemy. We urinated in the barrel. With our combined efforts it broke loose. Boblo began firing, cutting a wide swath of destruction. As he did I crawled back to Hildebrand.

When I looked back I could see Brinker sitting in the hole beside Boblo. He was reloading the clips which Boblo was rapidly expending.

"How does it work?" I yelled.

"It stinks!" came the reply from Brinker.

"What do you want, eggs in your beer?" asked Hildebrand, making sure that he got his say in this batch of humor.

Before an hour had passed, we realized that our position here was hopeless against such overwhelming odds. We thought of withdrawing, but it would be a slaughter, for we would have to expose ourselves to the dozens of automatic weapons which the enemy possessed.

The enemy moved in close. They were ready for the kill. We were trapped.

I looked over at Boblo. He was jumping his automatic rifle from one position to another in a series of quick movements. In each position, he fired a few rounds, while Brinker still reloaded the clips and occasionally threw a hand grenade. It added to the rattle and chatter of the small-arms fire.

In the last moment of decision, our own artillery was called in upon us. As it started, most of the small-arms firing ceased. We huddled in our holes, trying to push our shoulders up into our helmets. I could only be thankful that I was not a German soldier, that I did not have to face the American artillery day in and day out for so many long months.

Large, brown holes appeared in the surrounding snow, and geysers of frozen clods spouted up. Much of it rained down upon us. A near-by explosion nearly buried Hildebrand and me. When I looked up again, I could see the remains of someone splattered over the trunks of the surrounding trees. Quickly I looked over at Boblo and Brinker. They still huddled in their hole. I stretched my neck to look at the others, but everyone seemed to be alive.

As the shells continued to scream in, I could hear the cries and moans of wounded and dying men. They must have been the enemy, for the Americans cried very little. I wondered how long this would continue and if I would live through it. I was scared, ever so scared, but I did not know of what. I was not afraid of death; in fact, sometimes I had thought that I would have welcomed it. If I had to die, I would have liked to have had an hour to wind up my affairs.

Before long the artillery stopped. The enemy rushed upon us again, and we were ordered to withdraw. The Battle of the Bulge was on.

At first it was an orderly retreat, but before long we were forced to flee more rapidly. The enemy charged behind us, swarming through the trees in great numbers. Some rode heavy Tiger tanks, singing and shouting as they came. Many were dressed in black uniforms trimmed in red.

Hildebrand and I dived into a clump of bushes, and from this concealment we picked off some of the more jubilant ones riding on top of the tanks. For every one we hit, there was a dozen more to take his place.

The first wave swept by, but still we had to remain hidden. Another wave followed and still another. They were all well-built young men, armed to the teeth with the finest equipment.

After nightfall we decided to make our way in the direction our troops had fled. We moved quietly and cautiously, not knowing what lurked behind the trunk of the next tree. The greatest fear was of the mines that our troops could have left.

A trip wire caused us to set off a flare. We flattened ourselves out and waited for it to go out. It seemed to burn for ages. When it had burned out, we set a swift pace, just as the mortars began to drop all about it.

We made our greatest distance in the night, for during the daytime we had to remain hidden. Here we had to be careful. In France the civilians would have hidden us and helped us, but here everyone was against us.

We wandered in a general westward direction, keeping under cover as much as possible. We dared not follow paths and roads or go through towns, but had to travel cross-country through the fields and ditches. It was hard going and very tiring, especially without sleep and on an empty stomach.

Starvation must be a horrible way to die. We had

gone three days with one ration between us, and already I had tightened my belt several times. Now it did no good. My stomach was tight and felt collapsed—as if its sides were touching.

We talked it over. Something had to be done soon, for we became fatigued very quickly. Should we run onto the enemy we might not be a match for him.

A horse, killed in the recent engagement, lay in an open field. I cut a good-sized slab from the hind quarter, Hildebrand slipped it under his arm, and we dashed off. We had to keep moving, should someone be following us. Abandoned vehicles littered the countryside, cold, deserted, and covered with snow.

The sky was overcast, so we decided on a fire in an abandoned shack in a wood. In my helmet, with the aid of Hildebrand's bayonet, we stewed the pieces of horse flesh in water of melted snow. We took turns standing guard outside the building.

The odor of the boiling meat was not the most pleasant that I had ever known, but our aching hunger made the saliva flow freely.

When it was cooked, we wolfed it down. Sweet and stringy, it was still one of the most worthy meals we had eaten—it drove starvation a bit farther away.

I replaced my helmet on the liner. It was black and the straps were burned off, so I wedged it on, using the camouflage net to take up the slack. We moved on.

It was dark and foggy when we approached the battle line. Our greatest problem would be to distinguish enemy troops from our own, for we had to yell at the Americans to prevent them from firing on us, but we could not make a sound if the troops were enemy.

Once an enemy platoon, marching in formation, passed within six feet of us. At first I wanted to call out in hope that they were American, but the sound of a hobnail on a stone made me know that they were enemy. The Americans, and only the Americans, wore soft, quiet, cushioned rubber on their shoes. It made even the most clumsy soldier quiet and surefooted. Dozens of times I had thanked God that as an American soldier I was outfitted and backed by a land of plenty.

Quickly but quietly we slipped down a wide firebreak in the great forest. We avoided the places where two or more firebreaks intersected, for we knew that they were shelled every few minutes by both sides. This prevented any great movement of troops or equipment. Boblo always referred to them as "Purple Heart Junction."

Suddenly the silhouette of a soldier loomed up before me. I stopped in my tracks. Hildebrand was behind me and without looking I reached for his hand and squeezed it hard. By returning the squeeze, he let me know that he understood.

We could not afford to be exposed now that we were so close to being back to our line, so I decided not to bother to find out the nationality of the soldier on guard. Stooping low and moving swiftly, we attempted to go out around him.

Before we were halfway around he discovered us.

"Halt!" he shouted.

We stopped—frozen in our tracks, legs like jelly up to the hips.

He called out something in German.

"Yah! Yah!" I called back disgustedly, as if I were

busy and did not want to be disturbed. We moved off once again.

He sang out something again. This time the tone of his voice was a bit more mild.

We stopped. I could feel my hair raise on my neck.

"Moment!" I told him in a rather hush-hush tone.

Once again we moved on. This time we traveled by leaps and bounds, for no longer could he be stalled off. This was the real get-a-way.

When we came to a place we were sure was just a few yards from the American lines we stopped to wait for daylight.

"What happens if it's the enemy?" asked Hildebrand in a whisper.

"Two more telegrams will be sent to two more mothers," I whispered back. "I'll never be captured, and it will be sure suicide for two battered scouts to take on a whole kraut company."

When it was light enough, I tried to maneuver for a good look at the entrenched soldiers. Two rifles barked out. Twigs and bark flew about my head. They were M-1 rifles, for I could tell them anywhere.

"Hey! Are you Americans?" I cried out.

"You damn right we're Americans!" came the reply.

"Hold your fire! So are we!" I shouted back.

"Come out with your hands up!"

We left our rifles and slowly rose and walked forward with our hands raised high. I expected them to allow us to drop our hands and pick up our rifles after they had a good look at us, but they did not. We were treated like prisoners.

All of our ammunition was taken, and our rifles were

emptied before they were handed back. No one would listen to our protests.

"What company are you from?" asked a lieutenant.

"Company F," I answered.

"Regiment?" he continued.

Hildebrand told him.

"Go with this fellow," said the lieutenant, pointing to another rifleman.

At the command post we were interrogated by a clean-shaven major. He fired questions at us.

We showed our identification tags, gave the capital city of our state, and told him who won the world series. Still he seemed doubtful.

"Why all of this nonsense?" I asked. "After answering all of these questions why do you still think we are Germans?"

He leaned forward in his chair, "Because German soldiers, dressed in American uniforms, have been coming through the lines, just as you did. They had plenty of identification, dog tags, and could answer most of the questions you did. Their English was perfect. They create a lot of confusion and commit actual murder behind our lines. We cannot be too careful."

"Then you still think we are Germans?" asked Hildebrand.

"Well, not exactly," answered the major. "I have never seen any as dirty looking as you two, and most of them wear division insignia and rank on their sleeves." Then he continued, "But your complexion and names definitely point to German origin."

"Why don't you ask Company F about us?" I suggested.

"We'll take you there—what's left of it."

"Please give us a ration or two, major," I begged him. "We have had very little to eat for a week."

He gave us three rations each, and we tore into them.

As he watched us gobble them up, he chuckled a bit, "Going to have to shave one of these days, aren't you?"

"Sure am," Hildebrand sputtered. "Have a terrific catch of dandruff in my beard."

"It's even in my eyebrows," I added.

When we reached the company they were dug in outside a small town from which they had just been evicted. It still burned.

I found Charley—my old buddy—Charley Kruse. His beard and clothing were in the same shape as mine, and his eyes were red with fatigue. He was still the ammunition bearer for a light machine gun. I told him my story.

"Never thought I'd see you again," he said with a wide grin.

Then I spotted Boblo. He shared his hole with some-one new, for Brinker was missing in action. No one knew what had happened to him. The new fellow was as nutty as Boblo. He had worked in a New York the-ater, so in short order he put on a performance.

He stood and clapped his hands. "On stage girls—five minutes!" he stated with dignity. Then he pro-ceeded to give the chorus girl jig while humming an appropriate tune.

Two bullets whined past and returned us quickly to the grim realization of war and that we were now on the receiving end, that our company had been beaten to its knees and whittled to half its size.

For two days we held off every attack the enemy threw at us for we had been ordered to hold this point at all costs.

The ground was pitted with shell craters and the snow was buried beneath the frozen earth, pulverized by the constant pounding. At times the pitch of battle became so great that we had to call our own artillery upon us. At other times we crawled up close to the enemy holes to escape the shelling they were giving us. Often, upon returning, we found our foxholes blown into large craters by direct hits. Huge tanks came at us. Some were stopped, but many sped on. I chewed a piece of gum so fast that it became very warm and sticky. The heat must have come from the gum itself, rather than from my body, for my cheeks were cold inside as well as out.

One morning we were ordered to storm and capture the little town. The entire line was planning on moving up.

Four times we entered the town, and four times we were thrown back. Each time we withdrew a few more men were left lying in the streets and on the sidewalks. As the tanks rumbled in and out they crushed many. One man's head had been smashed so flat that it was over two feet in diameter. Another's leg got caught in a tread and slapped about as the tread turned.

The fifth time we stormed the battered town our outfit became separated. Things seemed confused. Even the enemy was disorganized.

I sprawled out on the sidewalk and fired at a sniper in the steeple of the village church. I fired six rounds, and he fell to the doorsteps below.

As I rose to my feet, another enemy soldier dashed around the building before me. By firing from the hip I dropped him with the two remaining shells in my rifle. He came to a sliding halt in a crumpled heap at my fcct.

Before I could reload, a second soldier lumbered around the corner. Quickly, I tossed my rifle aside and lunged at him. Before he could recover from the surprise he was on his back with my thumbs deep in this throat. He gurgled. His eyes pleaded with me; they spoke more loudly than any mouth. But my heart was hard with battle; it knew no sympathy. As the strength left my hands, life left his body.

When his body no longer throbbed with life, I jumped up, grabbed my rifle, and reloaded it. To make sure he would cause no further trouble, I fired a round into his forehead.

I looked up in time to see a middle-aged woman in the next block pouring boiling water into the face of a fallen American soldier. Without hesitation or deliberation, I fired three shots and she dropped to the street. The still-steaming kettle clattered loudly.

I rushed up to the fallen soldier. It was Hildebrand, his lips parted into a near-smile. His heavy beard showed off a fine set of teeth. I knew that I was crying, but I did not want to admit it—not even to myself. The battle raged about me, but I did not know it. I could feel nothing; I only knew that Herman Hildebrand, second scout of Company F, had been killed and scalded in this small German town near the Belgian border on this Christmas day of 1944.

I looked about and saw that the streets were barren and empty. An American machine gun chattered a few blocks to the right, so I broke into a trot and headed in that direction in hope of getting together with some other American soldiers.

As I approached the machine gun I could see that it was being manned by an enemy crew. I whirled about and started in another direction, but still my brothers-in-arms were nowhere to be seen.

After searching in vain for some time, I stumbled onto a dazed enemy soldier. He readily surrendered. He did not wear the black uniform.

At last, in desperation, I took the prisoner into an abandoned basement to await further development of the situation. Here I would hold my prisoner until more Americans came to give me confidence and protection. I only hoped that it would be the Americans and not the enemy.

I made the prisoner seat himself at a table, with instructions to keep his hands upon the table top at all times. Then I propped myself in a chair against the opposite wall.

Before long I decided to eat a ration. As I unwrapped it, I could see the prisoner's eyes light up and his mouth begin to water. It might be better for me to share it with him, should his comrades come, rather than mine.

We had no water for the bouillon powder, so I sprinkled it on the cheese. He ate it and smacked his lips as though it were a great delicacy. Apparently he had had no good food, especially chocolate, for a long time. He told me that he was very thankful for this

192

genuine food, for his food had been black bread, ersatz coffee, and simulated chocolate.

I stared at him but said nothing, for my mind was occupied in another direction. I thought I should shoot him, then go out in search of my company.

For a full hour I sat there and stared at my captive, pondering over the situation. The prisoner continued to eye me with an untiring vigilance. Perhaps he was plotting against me.

At that time I sat astride the fence of decision. Just a little push from one side or the other would have determined the fate of the prisoner. In legal circles it would have been classified as murder to shoot him. Besides, it would have been a very unfair match, for he had no weapon. But then again there was no such thing as fairness in warfare; the army indoctrination had taught me that. It taught me to cheat, kill, and fight in the foulest manner ever conceived by man. Never give the enemy a fair chance, for he would never give me one. Even at this time he was infiltrating our lines by wearing our uniforms. He had turned our weapons upon us and had strafed and bombed us with our planes. Once, when the enemy did not have time to take care of prisoners properly, they were herded into a group and machine-gunned to death.

Being inactive for a length of time caused me to become a bit drowsy. A sudden fear seized me. If I should doze off, I was sure my captive would have made sure that I awakened no more.

I jumped to my feet and fingered the trigger of my rifle. The prisoner raised his hands before his face and pleaded, "Nay! Nay!"

Quickly I brought the rifle to "port arms," dashed out the door, and silently slipped through the dying town. I no longer looked for a fight but dodged and hid. I only wanted to find the rest of the company.

When I found them, they were holding out in some houses on the outskirts. Captain Slye slapped me upon the back and then grabbed my arm. After looking up and down his dark circled eyes settled upon mine.

"Look, Frank," he began, "I want you to go back and pick up some rations and ammunition. I don't care where you get them or how you get them, but just make sure you do get them."

I nodded my head.

"I guess things are a bit tough," I mumbled.

"Tough, hell!" he shouted. "I'll decide when things get tough around here! I'll let you know when it gets tough! Now you get going and get those supplies, even if you have to hold up the Quartermaster Depot in Paris. But be damn sure you're back tonight. Here, leave your rifle and take this forty-five."

After taking off all bandoleers of ammunition and laying down my hand grenades, I started off on the run. When I had covered a mile or better, I came upon a highway. It was easier traveling and I made better time.

A ride in a jeep took me well out of range of artillery. When back far enough to have the traffic fairly heavy, I got out on a crossroad. The jeep driver looked at me rather suspiciously, but said nothing as he drove off.

There I waited and watched for a truck bearing the proper commodity.

It seemed ages before the right one came along, but when it did, I jumped on. Quickly, I squeezed through the canvas door and climbed into the seat beside the driver, a colored lad wearing a sheep-lined coat.

At first he wanted to halt the truck, but by holding the forty-five in my lap I convinced him to continue. Then I explained that no harm would come to him; that I was perfectly sane, but my company was desperate for supplies.

He said nothing but stared at the battle-scarred highway and nodded his head in nervous approval. It was getting dark and the artillery flashed like distant lightning. It created a continuous rumble.

Everything went well until the enemy artillery began to crash into the woods ahead. The driver jammed on the brakes and brought the truck to a skidding halt.

"Dis is as fah as ah go!" he screamed.

I put the forty-five against his neck, "Come on, get this thing moving before I let you have it!"

He stared at the bright flashes of the artillery. The tears streamed down his cheeks.

"No, suh," he muttered through quivering lips.

"Okay then, get out," I ordered him. "I'll take it from here."

He slipped out and quickly disappeared down the road.

I jammed the truck into gear and started off up the road. Before long the terrain became very familiar, and I had to leave the highway and take a narrow, winding road to the town the company was holding. I had to be very quiet to avoid drawing artillery fire.

I put the truck in low gear and let the motor idle. The noise it made was negligible.

There was only a mile to cover in this manner, but

it seemed terribly long. I held my breath and breathed in gasps, listening for anyone approaching or climbing into the truck. I listened for the shots of snipers and the scream of incoming artillery. I was bathed in nervous sweat, thinking of the mines which might have been planted in the road. Several times I got the urge to open the truck up and race it in, but my better judgment told me not to do it. I aged ten years in the half-hour it took.

Once within our guarded area, I drove the truck into a garage, then went to report to Captain Slye. He was very happy. With great formality, he poured two big drinks of liquor. Together we drank them in honor of the coming day in which we, Company F, were to clear the town of the remaining diehard SS boys—the black suited elite guard of the SS Panzer Division—the Deathhead Brigade.

We pushed on, house to house, street to street, and shoulder to shoulder. Often it went as a football game; at first we gained a few hundred yards, only to be thrown back a thousand yards a bit later. The snow hampered operations by holding up our tanks. A slight incline on the road made them slip and slide into the ditch so that we had to advance without them. Often we ran upon tough opposition which they would have helped us to easily overcome, but they were far behind.

We were fighting a special type of enemy with special equipment, for they were a choice group, chosen and equipped just for this particular push, the best array of manhood and equipment that I had ever seen. Yes, we were well fed and equipped, but they had a match for everything we had, and it usually went one better. Our semi-automatic rifle fired eight rounds before it had to be reloaded; they had one very similar, but it fired ten rounds. Our machine gun fired four hundred and fifty rounds a minute; theirs, fifteen hundred. Their seventy-five-ton tank had to be outnumbered by our thirty-three tonner at least three to one before there was an even chance for battle.

The soldiers of this enemy outfit were strictly die-hards. They fought to the death, even in a hopeless situation, instead of surrendering. They had had special training and indoctrination, and now wore special black uniforms, highly decorated with pink trimming. Their bayonets were of chrome, with bright black handles. Upon each handle was a metal skull and crossbones. They wore the same ornament on the collar of their tunic, and each had a skull and crossbones ring, with his individual initials and the lightning SS carved into it. Nearly all carried automatic weapons. Even the typewriter that we captured had a key with the SS on it.

As we battled our way back into the wooded area we passed over hundreds of bodies of American soldiers who had fallen as the onrushing enemy swept through a few days before. Their frozen bodies had caused the snow to drift into ridges following the contour of the body. Each one on his back had a very distinct drift ridge from his nose and each of his lips.

I came upon one which had not been drifted over, for he had died within the last day or two, perhaps from starvation or exposure. I could see that the tracks which led to the body were very crooked. He apparently had staggered this far, dropped, and had died. The eyelashes were frosted and his parted lips were filled with snow. His wrist watch was still running.

At night I stood guard among the towering pines. The big yellow moon had just risen, and once again my mind was occupied with a problem that had bothered me for as long as I could remember. Why did the moon seem larger when it rose? Once a college professor had told me that it was merely an optical illusion, but that had never satisfied my curiosity. There were many things I wanted to live and learn about.

The stars twinkled overhead. They had looked upon this earth for many years, but never had they witnessed such a mass destruction of men as well as machinery. I wondered if these stars would remember this scene, so they might persuade any other astrologer not to create another war of aggression.

IX.

IT was mid-January by the time we had battled our way back to the line held a month before. Then, and then only, did we hold up to wait for supplies and replacements.

When the replacements arrived, they did not meet our expectations.

"They're just kids," grunted Charley.

"After this last scramble, I guess they are scraping the bottom of the barrel. for replacements," added Boblo, with a shake of the head.

One of them was sent to share my hole as new second scout, filling the vacancy left by Hildebrand. I looked him over. His neatly pressed new clothing and shiny new field jacket hung on him like cheap rags. His frail body would never cause the seams to burst.

I looked up at him and saw he was bearded like a leopard. He hadn't shaved his shiny face for a month and need not again until spring. His blue eyes were soft and clear, but by the next week they would be a piercing red—a red of hate, of fear, and of tiredness.

I started up a conversation by introducing myself.

"Mine is Baker—Carlo Baker," he answered.

"Been over long?" I asked.

"Just landed at Le Havre four days ago. They shot us right up here."

"Yes," I said. "I guess they needed you up here all right. The going has been pretty tough lately."

He looked at me rather sorrowfully. "Sure wish they could have held off for another week. I'd have been able to spend Christmas at home. Wouldn't that have been nice?"

I stared out over the frosty terrain— Wouldn't Christmas at home have been nice. For me, Christmas had gone out when the war began. Each year it had found me farther away from home, and each year my situation had become steadily worse. This last yuletide season had been the darkest, saddest Christmas that a human being could comprehend—chilled to the marrow, half starved, and surrounded by an enemy who would rather kill than capture.

Even at this time, after I had survived that terrible ordeal, there still was no future. It was like being in an area plagued with a deadly contagious disease. There was no way out; it had to come sooner or later.

As time went on, I watched Baker perform his routine of precautions against the ills that might befall one on the front. He stimulated his scalp with his fingers, brushed his teeth, and massaged the gums. Once each day he changed his socks. He was able to do this because he had three pairs, two of which he kept tucked in his shirt beneath his belt. He didn't wash them, for they hardly had time to become dirty. I had two pairs, one of which I kept up in the head harness of my helmet liner, along with a few pieces of precious toilet tissue. I washed the socks whenever I was able. Often, however, it took them altogether too long to dry. Occasionally the kitchen crew collected all our spare socks and took them back for a good laundering. They were returned, clean and dry, within the next day or two. In this exchange there was no such thing as a good fit, for no one ever received his own socks back, and almost without fail, those with big feet were handed little socks and vice versa. No one complained or even tried to exchange with someone else; they merely rammed their feet into them and jammed back on their shoes.

"No, sir," Baker assured me. "No trench mouth or trench feet for me. I've read too much about it to be dumb enough to let it get a start on me."

The next morning he received a bullet right through the forehead. Yes, he had read all about trench mouth and trench feet, but somewhere along the way he had forgotten to read about raising his head above the level of the earth when the enemy was in view. No, I had never read it either, nor had anyone told me. I merely lived long enough to learn through experience and observation. Baker was not given that chance.

Long before, I had lost my curiosity for looking over the next hill or around the next corner. All too often it had proven too dangerous. There was plenty of trouble without looking for it.

For the next few weeks the new replacements were broken in by short skirmishes in the forest. Each day we pushed on a bit farther; each day the replacements felt the torments of being a combat infantryman. Every morning they awoke beneath a snowy blanket or sleeping bag, and tried to roll it into a neat bundle to sling over their backs, but it was an impossibility. It was a solid sheet of frozen snow and ice, so they cracked the ice and folded it in rough squares.

Each day they learned a bit more to harden them into ferocious fighters. Even I had learned a few new tricks the enemy was trying.

Ordinarily, at night, when we saw the tracer bullets of a machine gun arching up overhead, we would feel free to manuever about beneath them. Now, however, the enemy had synchronized another machine gun with it that fired without tracers. It raked a path just above the ground, thus getting the unsuspecting soldiers who were in its way.

After inching our way through the dark forest we came upon the great, bare, flat plains. Here we would hold until spring. We could not see the enemy, but we could feel him. He was entrenched in the earth, hidden in the strawstacks, and hiding in the basements of the towns which studded the area before us. We dared not venture into the open for fear of giving away our locations.

One evening, when the chow jeep and trailer brought up hot food, it also brought a few badges for the combat infantrymen of the outfit.

I, in turn, left my hole to go back and receive a mess kit full of hot corn, potatoes, and beef. As the peaches were heaped upon the top of this garbled mess a Combat Badge was slipped into my pocket.

After I had eaten, I sat in my hole and fingered the silver badge in the dim moonlight. What a way to receive such a treasured decoration. Often, in the United States, I had paraded and stood at attention for long periods, while Good Conduct Medals were pinned upon the breasts of soldiers who did not know how they had earned them. Perhaps they had managed not to get court-martialed for a year. This day I had received the Combat Infantryman Badge in a manner a dope fiend receives his fags from a peddler. I received it because I was fortunate enough to live through many months of physical and mental torture.

I opened my shirt pocket, attached it to the under side of the flap, and then rebuttoned the pocket. I would treasure it for the rest of my life. To me it was the highest decoration a soldier could earn. This was one medal I could proudly display without a thought of undeservingness. I would never have to bow my head when I stepped to the pay table for the extra ten dollars a month it would bring me. In my mind I knew how I had earned it and why I had received it, even if a cook had been the only witness of my receiving it.

Two new tanks had been attached to the company. They seemed bright and clean, but each had a rugged name printed in white letters on its side: "Lackanooky" and "Miss Carriage." To an ordinary audience this would have brought laughs and chuckles, but to us it brought hardly a smile. We only hoped they would be near to support us in the hour of need.

During a lull I slipped over to Boblo's hole. He was munching on a piece of K ration cheese, his wiry friend sitting beside him, a far different picture from when I had first met him. He looked tired and haggard, lean and wasted.

"Feel like giving the chorus-girl jig today?" I asked.

"Nope!" he replied. "This eighty-eight that I've been dancing to lately isn't a piano."

I turned to Boblo, "I wonder where Brinker is?"

"I don't know." He looked up at the sky, "Often I've thought about him. I hope he is either in good hands or is dead. This batch of Germans certainly wouldn't give him a prisoner's paradise."

Often there was talk of a "big push" or the "Spring push." We all understood that there must be another offensive, for we certainly couldn't beat the enemy by sitting here and waiting, but we felt much safer waiting than advancing. The uncertainity of waiting bore heavily upon our nerves.

To me, waiting was little better than advancing, because almost nightly I was called up to lead a patrol. Patrols were risky business, and at this time it was getting worse. The snow was not as heavy as it used to be, and the mines were beginning to worry me. Several times during the last few days I had seen some of the prongs which protruded from the ground. These prongs were the trip mechanism to a "bouncing betsy," a mine which, when sprung, jumped up two or three feet into the air before exploding. It fired bits of shrapnel in all directions, making it nearly an impossibility to escape once it had been set off.

Finally the great day came. Early in the morning we moved out on the great offensive. Spring was still over a month away, but still we called it the "Spring offensive."

We moved off down a macadam road in the gray of early dawn, hoping to catch the unsuspecting enemy dozing.

Suddenly, a low moan, which gradually rose to a

screaming whistle, broke the silence. The explosion knocked me across a ditch and into a field. The smell of sulphur irritated my lungs. I could hear men moaning to the rear where the shell had landed. It had nearly wiped out the second platoon.

After freeing myself of the wire fencing in which I was entangled, I bounced back onto the road. We moved out again, this time with a distance of thirty feet between each man. We could not afford to lose so many men from one shell.

At first it took considerable fighting to crack the enemy's defense lines, but as time went on, our great offensive gathered momentum. Never, at any time, did it roll as fast as we would have liked, however. Some of the villages were scarcely defended, while others gave us considerable difficulty. At times we were beaten down and driven back, but only as long as it took some artillery and armor to give us a supporting hand. Occasionally the Air Corps brought in its dive bombers.

There was always something to keep us from rolling too easily—a railroad, a forest, or a well-defended highway. On this particular day it was a river. They told us that two huge dams were still in enemy hands just up the river a short distance. Our company had been given the honor of liberating them.

"What a thing to fight over," said Boblo.

Yes, what a thing to fight over, but to me it made no difference. Since I had been over, I had seen us fight over everything from wine to windmills. A dam would just be something a bit different. It didn't excite me much, for it still was not a change from fighting. The day there was a change from that would be the day for me to get excited—the day that I could smile and breathe freely again.

"I wonder why we get the privilege of capturing it?" asked Boblo rather disgustedly. "They will probably have it heavily defended."

"They must think we are a bunch of good men," I told him. "Besides, it will be better to be up there than down here if they blow it up."

Under the cover of darkness we eased up to the dam. Its thundering roar beat at our eardrums throughout the night while we waited.

Long before the light of day we jumped the surprisingly small number of defenders. The battle was short and heated.

As the sun rose above the horizon we found ourselves in full possession of twenty-seven prisoners and a huge power dam. However, they managed to set off a small explosion before we could complete its capture. This small break would cause a mild flood below, but this wouldn't worry us. As we left the area, we gazed upon the vast area to our right.

"I feel sorry for those birds down there," said Boblo. "They're going to have to build a bridge or swim. We sure hit it lucky."

A short walk brought us to a very similar dam. This time the enemy was ready, for already he was shelling us.

We dropped to the ground and crawled, firing as we went. When we closed in, the enemy retreated across the top of the dam and then brought a murderous fire to bear upon us. They had a machine gun set up at their end of the walk across the top of the dam.

206

After half an hour of inching ourselves into a good firing position, Boblo and I drove the crew from the machine gun. One of our machine guns was set up in a similar manner at our end of the dam.

Under the protective fire of this weapon we crawled out onto the walk. Then the shells began to fall about us. At first it was small mortar shells, but soon the scream of the heavy artillery was added to the din. As each shell was pumped into the side of the huge dam, it seemed to jerk and shake; it felt as if it were made of soggy mud. From the size of the holes that the heavy shells made, I began to believe that the dam was made mostly of mud.

With this in mind, the roar of the falling water seemed even louder than the explosions of the bursting shells. What a place to be should the foundation be knocked out from under us. I looked over at Boblo hugging the walk, with huge beads of sweat on his forehead.

"Still feel sorry for those fellows?" I asked.

"Nuts!" came the reply.

We wormed our way across, while others followed close behind. At a given signal from our lieutenant we all jumped up and stormed the enemy. A few were taken prisoner but most retreated.

Once again we were assembled with our tanks, Miss Carriage and Lackanooky. Together we began the long drive across the level plains. No great barrier lay in our path for many, many miles.

The soft, warm sunshine melted the white blanket of winter. We slogged through the heavy mud, trying to keep the tanks on the hard-surfaced roads whenever possible. As the frost went from the ground, the mines were exposed. To many it gave relief; to others it was a constant reminder to be on the alert.

We were shelled constantly. There was no concealment, and the enemy could see us coming for miles. As the shells fell upon us, our planes roared overhead. They gave us confidence, but they could not stop the shelling. They strafed and bombed the enemy, but still we were shelled.

The enemy artillery and mortars were concentrated in the towns and villages that dotted the great plain. Long before we captured a town and silenced its guns we were being shelled by the next town. And so it went. There seemed to be no end.

For most of the towns and villages we had ample power to drive the enemy out, but occasionally, however, the resistance was more than we had bargained for. A working over by our howitzers usually gave us enough of an upper hand to take it.

While trying to take one of the larger cities, not too far from the mighty Rhine River, we came upon a very large and determined force of the enemy. We were thrown back several times, and each time it was shelled until the streets were gravelled with glittery, gray shrapnel, but still we could not enter.

At one point an abandoned streetcar rested upon its tracks in the middle of a sloping street. We loaded it hastily with captured shells stacked in a near-by warehouse, while the lieutenant prepared a time fuse. We lit it, released the brake, and gave the streetcar a start. Then we hid to watch the results of our scheme. We hoped that it would explode when it reached a barricade a few blocks farther on.

We watched it wobble and weave as it rolled down the empty street. Suddenly it lurched, jumped the track, and turned over on its side; the shells spilled out and rolled about. Our hope for its success faded. As we watched, a small pop and a puff of smoke let us know that the explosion we had wanted would never take place.

Once again we tried to advance, but were thrown back. Then we backed away from the city and waited.

The artillery began to pump more shells into the already smouldering city. Our dive bombers appeared by the dozens and began their pitiless bombing and strafing.

As we watched the city crumble before our eyes, the wind brought the smoke and stench to us. It was a sickening indescribable odor. I would never be able to forget the stench of a smouldering, dying city.

When we entered the city again, there were no streets to dash through, no cellars to clear out, and no buildings to obstruct the view. Heaps of glazed brick and mortar spread out as far as the eye could see. Occasionally a lone wall or chimney broke the ripple of the horizon. This was the most final job that I had yet witnessed.

As we scrambled up over the hundreds of small crests and through the many craters, only sporadic resistance remained to be overcome. Most of the enemy soldiers were dirty and dazed; no more fight remained in them. Their minds had been battered as badly as the city they so nobly defended.

Near the center of this mass of rubble that was once

one of the finest, most modern cities on the continent, hundreds of newly scattered pieces of paper littered the ground. They were of a pea-green color.

In the bottom of a crater, I picked one up and looked it over. It was an authentic-looking check filled in with a typewriter. It read: "No. 13; Philadelphia, February 25, 1945; The Philadelphia National Bank; Pay to the order of Your Widow, Ten Thousand only dollars." Then in the lower left corner: "10,000." It was signed with a heavy black signature. The title of the signer followed: "Major General, the Adjt. Gen., U.S. War Dept."

I shook my head in disgust. What a rotten way to fight a psychological war!

I turned the check over. There, written in a blue script, was more: "This will give your widow a chance to buy a new husband. His dowry will be your suits and things. Are you going to let this check be cashed?"

I gathered two, folded them neatly, and slipped them into my wallet. They would be fine souvenirs to carry home. They bothered me very little, but one could readily see that they were bound to have an effect upon some of the married men.

The highways in this part of Germany were some of the finest I had ever seen. We could not travel very fast because of mines and the breaks created by blown-up underpasses. We saw, however, that it would be much easier to maintain our lengthening supply lines on this type of highway, than it had been on the narrow, winding roads of France and Belgium.

Day after day we rumbled on. The tanks were becoming very plentiful. We liked that. They gave us plenty of firepower when we entered the numerous towns and villages. Often we watched tanks of both sides battle it out in the muddy fields. Our tanks greatly outnumbered the enemy's.

Often at night I stood guard beside a tank and talked with the driver or gunner. They called us gravel agitators. Whenever an infantryman was out of rations he could always get some from a tanker, for they carried them by the case. However, they all seemed to have one complaint in common: they wanted a forty-five rather than the submachine gun they had been issued. When their tank was hit, they had to get out before another shell ripped through it. There was no time to fumble about for a submachine gun. Many times I had seen them crawl from a crippled tank, only later on to cuss because they were unarmed.

Bloated and swollen animals lay dead in the fields. They lay on their backs and sides with their legs sticking straight out and far apart. Many of those still grazing had large, gaping holes in their bodies. Some had huge pieces of flesh gouged out, and an amber-colored fluid oozed from each wound and ran down their coats. Falling artillery frightened them and they dashed wildly about in their enclosures.

An enemy plane had been shot down in an open field near us. After it skidded to a stop in the mud, the pilot climbed out, shed a suit of coveralls, and stood with his hands on his hips.

Hurd, another scout, and I were ordered to bring him in, so we walked over with our rifles leveled. As we approached, he very dramatically removed a chrome trench knife and a pistol from his belt and placed them

211

upon the coveralls before him. We motioned for him to come with us.

In good English he replied very arrogantly, "I am a colonel, and I demand that I be taken prisoner by someone of at least that same rank."

I was not in a mood to be ordered about by an enemy, but perhaps he had something whereby he might have been of more value alive than dead. Hurd and I returned to the lieutenant and reported the situation.

"Come on," he snorted. "I'll go with you."

Together the three of us returned to the pilot. The lieutenant ordered him to come along, but he refused. The lieutenant shot him down.

Hurd slipped the aviator's watch from his wrist, and I took his fine leather gloves. This exposed a gold ring with a large diamond setting. I tried to slip it from the finger, but this was impossible, for it was much too small to pass over the knuckle. I stood, ready to walk away. The lieutenant, who had been standing over us, stooped down. With his bayonet he cut the finger off and removed the ring. We moved off.

I examined the gloves more closely. They were made of very fine material, and the workmanship was something that I had never seen before. There was a label inside the right-hand glove, "*Deutscher Lederhandschuh* —9." Should I be captured, it might cost my life. Then I thought: Me? Captured? Never! I promised myself before that I would never be taken prisoner.

At one point our squad was pinned down in a cabbage patch, and we were forced to crawl through the mud and slimy cabbage. The cabbages had been frozen all winter long, and now they were thawed and smelled very foul. The odor that got into our clothing was lasting and penetrating.

A machine gun was firing at us from a strawstack a couple hundred yards ahead. One of our riflemen stood, then ran a zigzag course toward it. He was trying to rush it, but when halfway there he was hit in the legs.

I looked back and saw that the machine gun which had been supporting us was being withdrawn into a small clump of brush and trees. Then the mortar shells began to drop among us. Each move we made drew fire from the strawstack. We were forced to withdraw.

I rushed into the clump of bushes in search of the machine gun which had been withdrawn, and when I found it, I saw that it was manned by a new replacement and a new second lieutenant.

"Where do you birds think you're going?" I stormed. "Don't you see that soldier out there bleeding to death because no one can get to him? Set that gun up and start firing."

"But the mortars are firing at us," stuttered the lieutenant rather meekly.

"Damn the mortars!" I raved.

"Okay! Okay!" he answered.

Boblo came up, "Will you keep me covered if I go after him?"

"You bet your life," I assured him.

He dropped his BAR and dashed out into the field. I lay upon my stomach and kept the bullets tearing into the strawstack, while the machine gun rattled beside me.

He put the wounded soldier over his shoulders and started back on the run. I could see the mud splatter about him as he lumbered back under the load. How he made it would never be explained through logic.

One of our tanks came up and set the strawstack on fire with its fifty-caliber machine gun. Boblo lay on the ground at its side, and when the enemy fled the burning strawstack he cut them down with his automatic rifle.

We reached the edge of the mighty Rhine. Here we had to wait, for there was no immediate way to cross. I had visions of rest, sleep, a bath, and warm food.

As I looked down upon the river, I saw the body of an American soldier resting upon the sandy edge. He had been washed up from the river. How did he get there? We were the first American soldiers to tread upon this area.

As I looked at him, I tried to make myself think that he was not dead, only sleeping. His downy face was soft and innocent looking; he was merely a child. He couldn't have been properly trained, for he hadn't had time to be polished by the sands of time. I thought that his mother should have known of his whereabouts, for he was not old enough to be out among strangers alone. Now, there he lay—beached.

A hand fell upon my shoulder. It was our lieutenant. Questioningly, I gazed into his tired and bloodshot eyes.

"They've captured a bridge intact upstream a couple of miles," he murmured. "We've been ordered to give them a hand."

I looked back at the dead soldier. That explained why he was there—killed upstream and had floated down. This was as far into Germany as he would get. I wondered if I would go farther.

214

When we came to the bridge, we took great intervals between men, for the shelling was terrific. It seemed to create a wall which was impassable.

The lieutenant led and I followed, while the shells continued to whine and whistle. It was a railway bridge, and the tracks gave the appearance of a hundred miles in length. Actually it was about five hundred yards.

As we jolted along, a shell broke an overhead cable. It swung down, hitting the side of my helmet, knocking me flat. My helmet fell into the swirling water far below. I jumped up and continued on my way.

Once across, we turned left down the embankment and pushed on. The resistance was not too great, but we had to make sure that each house was clear of the enemy.

At one place I entered a home where the family was eating the evening meal. They did not seem frightened like most. The man of the house laughed loudly and told me to quit my clowning and sit down for a bite to eat. I gritted my teeth and pointed the rifle at his head. This made him understand.

After they had all filed down the stairs into the basement I went through the rest of the house. The bathroom door was locked, so with the rifle butt I knocked it open. A woman sat in the tub in the process of taking a bath. I pointed the rifle at her and ordered her to get out and go into the basement. She protested and wanted me to leave until she had dressed, but I did not trust her, so I refused and more sternly demanded that she do as I commanded. With anger showing in her face, she got out of the tub and pounded her feet upon the floor. Her eyes glared, and she was not at all modest. Without taking time to dry herself she put on a robe and stamped her way to the basement, her flabby buttocks bouncing merrily as she went.

An armored infantryman had fallen in the street, and his helmet lay beside him. He would no longer need it, so I picked it up and placed it on my bare head. A helmet was not too much real protection, but it did have a good psychological effect.

In one small town we captured a brewery, a winery, and a fruit cannery, which lay on the eastern edge of the town by the railroad tracks. It was in these buildings that we spent the night on guard, and, of course, we had to sample their wares.

In the cannery there were burlap sacks of sugar stacked to the roof top. It was not fine granulated sugar, but as coarse as rock salt. Gallon cans of red jam were piled high in another corner. I was sure that after our cooks had discovered this we would eat red jam for many weeks to come.

We stopped following the river and again turned east—forever eastward. We entered the steep, forest-covered hills—the dark weird hills of the werewolves. The resistance was becoming very stiff, for at this time the enemy had become organized against the unexpected bridgehead. He had had time to bring men and equipment to face us.

We battled our way up and around. Time and again we tried to pass over the crest, but each time the overwhelming enemy force beat us back.

I looked back down upon the river to our rear. It was bright and shiny through the haze of smoke, and all roads leading to the bridge from the other side were choked with traffic of all descriptions. Vehicles and men continued to pass over its badly battered structure. It loomed up like the trunk of a huge tree being fed by osmosis.

Occasionally a shell put it out of commission. Each time I saw the flow of traffic stop my heart sank, for it was the only link between us and the supporting forces. To think that all of that massed equipment was so near yet unable to help us gave one a feeling of being cut off and surrounded that could have been experienced in no other position. In each case, however, the damage was repaired and the rows of loaded vehicles paraded on.

Several times lone German planes skimmed over the surrounding hilltops in a futile effort to dive bomb the bridge. They were fast, silent, and jet propelled. Each time one whined over we turned to watch it. It was met with such a barrage of antiaircraft fire that it was forced to drop the bomb haphazardly and flee. As it passed back over us, they continued to fire at it, giving us a good working over with the falling shells. At one time they set the grass on fire. We could not stand to fight the fire, so we merely allowed it to burn over our positions. From then on, our skirmishing made us as black as the ace of spades. Never before had I seen such white eyes and teeth with such black faces and bodies.

We dug in on the crest of the blackened hill in preparation for holding it, for we could advance no farther. During the course of the day we held back four infantry counterattacks supported by armor. They were paratroop fanatics who came charging at us in full battle fashion. Each time we held our fire until they were comparatively close. Then we opened up and cut them down or drove them back.

A German officer stood, yelled, and waved his arms wildly for his men to come forward.

"He's my meat!" yelled Boblo.

So we gave him the privilege of disposing of the raving officer.

Several times, when a tank would come at us, I watched a rifleman named Kelly jump up and run down the hill to our rear. Each time the tank would follow him past two old buildings which hid a waiting tank destroyer. Kelly would then yell to the tank destroyer as he ran past, thus alerting the crew. As the unsuspecting tank rumbled past, they fired a shell through it. Kelly would then turn, drop to the ground, and fire at the escaping crew of the tank.

As night closed over us, we were relieved. At first we had visions of a soft bed, or perhaps even a pass. All of this faded, however, when we went back a mere five hundred yards and dug in again. We did manage to get hot food, but still were kept awake by screaming, crashing, artillery shells.

Before dawn we were fed again, and then moved out. We passed through our old positions and on, as a thundering artillery barrage opened the way for us. As we advanced it continued to rise, always just a few hundred yards ahead. This rocked the enemy back on his heels.

Soon we were confronted with a small town upon a hill a mile distant. An open field lay between us and the town. The town overlooked an *autobahn*, so it was strongly defended.

At one point Boblo and I took refuge behind a dead horse. As the bullets splatted into the other side of the bloated carcass the gas hissed out.

"We've got to get out of here!" yelled Boblo. "One of those might come through."

We got up and began to run for the near-by road, for the ditch might offer us protection. A mortar shell dropped. The blast toppled me. A huge piece of shrapnel hit Boblo on top of his helmet, practically driving him down, but merely denting the helmet. He got to his knees and shook his head.

"Are you all right?" I asked.

"Yah, I think so," came the bewildered reply.

We dashed for the ditch.

Boblo rolled over on his back, "Look at me here," he said, pointing to a hole in his field jacket.

I tore open the field jacket and found a hole in his shirt pocket. I opened his shirt.

"No hole in the undershirt," I told him with relief.

I reached into the pocket and pulled out his wallet and Combat Badge. The badge was badly bent. The piece of shiny shrapnel was wedged partially through the wallet.

"You were lucky," I told him, as I showed them to him.

"But it sure hurts," he insisted.

We entered the town while our artillery continued to pound it. The going was hard, and the casualties were high, but we captured several times our number in prisoners. The dead of both sides lay in the hay lofts, wheelbarrows, and back yards—wherever they were killed or wherever, when wounded, they ran to die. I watched one enemy machine gunner beaten to death with his own weapon because he was known to have inflicted several casualties upon us.

I heard a slight rustle in the basement of a house I was approaching, so I yelled for them to come out. I heard nothing, so I fired three shots into the window. Up the stairs came a little girl with her hands over her head. It made me feel embarrassed and ashamed. In my mind I tried to validate my actions by telling myself that safety's sake demanded such precautions. I gave the girl a stick of gum and continued.

I received a bullet through the helmet. It came from an angle so that it entered the front and should have passed right back out an inch or so farther on. Once on the inside, however, the contour of the helmet had caused it to continue on the inside for six inches before it passed out again. To look at the outside of the helmet one would have thought that it must have passed through my skull.

I went to the medical aid man to have him pull the steel shavings from the scalp on the side of my head. They had been peeled from the helmet by the bullet as it slid along the inside.

Two days later we were relieved by another division. They seemed surprised at the small number of us who marched so wearily away. We were weary because, being so few, we had had to stand guard most of the time.

When we were reinforced again a platoon of negroes was added to our company. The lieutenant in charge of them was not colored. At first we were skeptical, but they soon proved themselves to be worthy infantrymen.

Our objective was a small woods in which we were to

spend the night before making an assault upon a town ahead. The woods were filled with enemy soldiers. At first, we were driven back to the ditch on the far side of a near-by *autobahn,* so we decided to take it by marching fire.

We filed through an underpass, fanned out, and began firing from the hip. We fired with every third step, at anything that moved. The machine gunners held their weapons in the same manner and fired them in short bursts. The belts of ammunition had been cut into four-feet lengths and dangled down to the ground. On the gunner's left hand was a leather mitt to protect it from the heat of the barrel. Occasionally, I looked down at my rifle and saw that the barrel was purple from the heat. The surrounding wood was smoking and dripping grease.

We took the woods in short order, wounding but one of our men. We found one dead enemy.

In a few minutes our fighter planes appeared and strafed and bombed the little wooded plot. The tops fell from the trees, the trunks turned white as bark was ripped from then, and the bombs ripped huge holes in the ground. I could hear the radioman yelling and pleading over the radio to have them called off. Apparently higher headquarters had thought we needed help to take the woods and did not know that we were already in them.

Our faithful friend, the little artillery observation plane, came in and hovered above us, thus foiling the attempts of the fighters to come down again. He knew the lines as no other one did. For this we were forever grateful. The time he allowed was time enough to save us, as well as to call off the other planes. Often he had told us of an approaching enemy company or of a hidden enemy tank, thus giving us a warning. At one time he took a case of hand grenades and tossed them at entrenched enemy infantry.

Morning found us making our way toward the town which lay in a valley on the turn of a river. Along the ditches and in the open fields our artillery and tanks did a wonderful job of disposing of a bitter, entrenched, and determined enemy. The dead soldiers lay in the ditches, head to heel. To make sure that they were not playing dead, we pushed the end of the rifle barrel into an eye. If he did not move, we were certain that he was dead. One went so far as to put a hole in his helmet to make us think he was dead, but he was discovered.

At one place an enemy soldier was moaning. Beside him one could see where an artillery shell had made a direct hit on one of his comrades. There was no part of him that remained as large as my hand, and the entire ground was covered with red bits of ground flesh for a radius of fifteen feet.

A colored soldier went over to the moaning enemy and put him out of his misery. It was better, for there would have been no hope for him. He would merely have suffered on a few more hours.

When we entered the town, we found it infested with snipers. The enemy, who had been watching us descend into the town from the hills across the river, poured the shells upon us. We took refuge in a warehouse, where we found German army field rations. They did not interest us because they tasted so artificial—almost everything was simulated.

Throughout the day we fought our way through the town. The high-caliber shells came in so fast that we could watch the town crumble building by building. We saw homes ripped in half so as to give a regular cross-section view; the furniture seemed to all be in place. Others just collapsed into the basement.

"I have an idea on building houses," said Boblo, with a twinkle in his eye. "Just build a basement and fill it with materials, then you will know you have enough to complete the house."

"Where did you get that bright idea?" I asked.

"Well, here it works in reverse. The whole house fits into the basement, when properly arranged."

We laughed. What a way to create satire!

As the dusk of evening came we had cleared the town, with the exception of a cemetery on the edge. As we started toward it, I went over to investigate a track-laying tractor used in pulling heavy guns. It seemed abandoned. The back portion, made of a framework covered over with a tarpaulin, was used to carry ammunition. With the muzzle end of my rifle, I pried apart the slit in the curtain which hung down over the back. A bayonet on the end of a rifle shot out, missing my throat by inches. I jumped back. Then I emptied two clips, of eight shots each, into the tarpaulin and left to join the others who were fighting in the cemetery.

The light was fading rapidly from the sky, making it hard to see. Behind each large tombstone lurked a die-hard enemy soldier who leaped at me with a fixed bayonet. To me a bayonet was made only to open tin cans and to scrape the mud from one's boots. I would never use one, for bullets were so much easier and cleaner.

223

The artillery from both sides came in upon us, and huge hunks of marble and granite flew about like little stones. The flashes glittered back and forth on the shiny, broken tombstones. The area was full of human bones, hair, and rags. Pine boards were uprooted and smashed to splinters.

The next day we were to remain in the town, so Boblo and I went to the cemetery to search for jewelry. We could find none. Perhaps it was so hard to see and find because it was tarnished.

We stood over one shattered grave and tried to read the epitaph on the broken tombstone. We made out the name and the usual, "May he rest in peace."

Boblo looked about at the scattered bones and rags.

"May he rest in peace," he repeated. "That's what it used to be. When they make up the new tombstone, they'll have to make it read: 'May he rest in pieces.' That's awful, isn't it?"

"Yes," I agreed. "These people died once, and now they have been uprooted and killed again."

Each move we made in the open brought mortar fire from the hills across the river, so I sat in the shadows of some trees and looked about. It was spring, but nothing showed it; everything seemed to have been killed. The finger of destruction had touched everything. Spring ordinarily brought life, but only death abided here. Perhaps things would just remain dormant until it was over. Then the birds would return and sing, and the grass would become green, and the flowers would bloom.

An elderly man, the caretaker of the cemetery, had burdened himself with the task of collecting the dead and burying them. After each was put away, he took a large swig of liquor. After half a dozen trips he was feeling so high he came over and sat beside me.

"I'm tired," he said. "If the rest of them want to get buried, they'll have to come over here themselves."

I looked into his eyes. He did not smile. I grinned a bit and looked away. Such a dry sense of humor!

Boblo and I were requested to go back in search of the mortar squad which should have been supporting us but had not been heard of for the past twenty-four hours.

After searching for several hours, we found the entire squad dead in a small ravine about a mile from town. They had been ambushed and machine gunned to death, probably by some enemy soldiers we had by-passed in the surrounding hills and woodlands.

For several minutes we stood and stared at their bodies sprawled about down the little ravine. Their guns and shells were scattered about with them. Most of them were curled up on their sides or doubled up on their knees and elbows, with their faces in their helmets.

"They're pretty young, aren't they?" said Boblo solemnly.

"None of them have reached twenty," I added.

We continued to look down upon their fuzzy faces and oversized uniforms—uniforms made for men.

"How old do you think I am?" asked Boblo, without looking up.

"Twenty-two?"

"I'm nineteeen."

That night, six of us, including two negroes, were to go on a combat patrol across the river. We were to locate and silence a heavy gun which had been harassing us.

We turned in everything, except government-issued equipment, to the lieutenant. Our weapons were of our own choosing. I kept my rifle and picked up a trench knife and a piece of piano wire with a wooden handle on each end. The negroes took a well-sharpened bayonet and a light submachine gun, or greasegun, as we called it.

The lieutenant produced a map and briefed us: "You are here in Hennef-on-the-Sieg. You are to cross the river and go up into these hills. The gun is right here. You are to be finished and on your way back by 0300. Now, should you run into too much trouble, get back into this area here and fire three tracers straight into the air. An observer, who will be waiting on this side of the river, will radio our artillery and mortars. They will box you in until we can get you out of there."

Some of the others questioned him about certain details. I checked and adjusted my equipment.

"What's that wire for?" asked one of the colored soldiers.

Before I could answer Boblo cackled out, "He's going to commit a G String murder."

With great difficulty we swam the swift river. Then we made our way slowly but silently up the wooded hills. Several times we came upon small groups of enemy soldiers and were forced to detour. Each time we had been warned by their talking, their smoking, or the noise from their hobnailed boots.

Several times I looked back at my two negro companions. They were among the bravest soldiers with whom I

226

had ever patrolled. They were both well educated and had given up much of their rank to volunteer for the infantry. They went over well on night patrols, for when they closed their mouth and eyes it was impossible to see them. I could see an occasional glisten from the shiny bayonets they held in their teeth.

Before long we came upon the gun we were searching for. We separated into pairs and worked our way toward it. With my colored companion right upon my heels I silently slipped up behind a dozing sentry, formed a large loop in the piano wire, slipped it over his head, and then pulled with all my strength. As it cut into his throat, I could feel his body become limp. Quickly I removed it, threw his pistol away, and we moved on.

We squatted and waited while two of our comrades placed a charge in the breach of the mighty weapon. Before it could go off, however, others of the crew had been awakened, and we had a terrific battle on our hands. In the confusion we all managed to flee safely, but the enemy was hot upon our trail.

We reached the designated spot, fired the tracers, and then turned to bring fire upon our pursuers. In a matter of seconds the shells started to fall on all four sides of us; artillery to the front and left, and mortars to the right and rear. Even the large shells of the corps artillery were coming in.

In the morning the shelling ceased, and a large combat team, armed to the teeth, came to the rescue and escorted us back.

Along the river bank, six prisoners were taken. One of our soldiers collected their rifles and proceeded to throw the entire lot into the rapidly flowing river. Suddenly he turned about, a look of amazement covered his face; he had thrown his own rifle in with them.

The mail arrived, and I received several stained letters and a badly battered Christmas package. There was explanation on each in pencil: "Recovered from sunken ship."

The ink on the letters had soaked through the stationery in a very orderly fashion. It had not run at all, but merely had made a very legible inscription upon the back of each sheet. Those which had been written on both sides were impossible to decipher.

The package contained cookies, candy, and peanuts. The cookies were spoiled and candy dissolved into a mushy ball. The peanuts could be eaten, but they were the saltiest salted peanuts I had ever eaten. I took them upstairs to share with the artillery observer, who was sitting in the attic of the three-story house we had taken as our quarters. I shoved the bag under his nose, and he grabbed a handful.

"Thanks," he grunted, as he rushed to the small opening at the front end of the building. He watched to see where the phosphorous smoke shell he had just called for would land.

"What are you trying to hit?" I asked.

"The source of the twelve shells that whistle over here every fifteen minutes."

"Why, they're landing near that church right behind us. You can almost reach out and grab one as they go over."

He sat down and scratched his greasy head. Still

228

munching the peanuts, he studied the map spread out on the floor.

"If I ever locate them, I'll blow them off the map," he growled. "Even the old man's getting tired of my wasting shells while trying to find them."

"Why, what does he have to say?"

"He tells me to stick my head out the window when they pass over and try to sense the direction they're coming from."

We both laughed at that, for it sounded like some brass hat. One day up here would have changed his mind. It didn't always happen as it was written in the rule book for that book was written by another brass hat who received his information by reading other books. A bit of experience would have given them enough information to give back a sensible answer.

A chaplain came up to say mass. He was of slim stature and had a head full of black hair, cut off in a brush-like fashion. He chose an abandoned machine shop for the ceremony.

His face was taut. From his thin lips came a short sermon telling us to remember that God was forever present and was on our side, even if, at times, it didn't seem that way.

The shells came in again, but the chaplain didn't flinch a muscle, even though some of the shrapnel came through the window and dribbled across the floor. The entire mass took twenty minutes. When it was over he shook hands with us and said that he would pray for us every day. As we left, his eyes followed us. He knew that we wouldn't all be back for the next mass.

We were issued a change of new clothing. All seemed

normal except for the trousers. They had full seats, as if they had been tailored for women, and created the saddest-looking company of soldiers that one could imagine. The crotch of everyone's pants hung to his knees, and we called each other "bloomer boy," or "droopy drawers."

A few minutes after we were in our new clothing, a runner brought awards for two soldiers of our company. The two awards were to go to Kelly and Boblo.

Kelly received the Bronze Star for gallantry in action. The action was described as that when Kelly led the enemy tanks down the hill to the waiting tank destroyer.

Boblo received a Certificate of Merit for rescuing the wounded soldier who had been hit by the machine gun hidden in the strawstack back on the open plains. It was merely a piece of paper the shape and size of an ordinary diploma.

We moved out, crossed the river, and began pushing the enemy back. The line was stretched so thin that we sometimes bypassed small groups of the enemy holding out in some isolated spot. All three rifle companies of our battalion were on line, instead of one being in reserve to assist the others which might run into stiff opposition. We were told that we had to fight our way out of anything we got into, for there was no one to call on for help.

Sometimes we cleared a town and moved on up the hill ahead, in preparation for descending upon the next little village. While we were on the hill, the town which we had just cleared would be filled again with enemy soldiers. They had fled from the towns to our left and right which were being cleared by the other companies. It was then that we had to tighten our belts and fight like tigers, for we were on top of a hill and surrounded on all four sides.

Once when entering a town I was pinned down in the gutter and forced to remain there for half an hour while the bullets whined overhead and sparked on the street about me. Boblo had always kept me covered and had gotten me out of situations like this, but this time he did not come.

When I was free again, I set off in search of Boblo. I found him sitting in the middle of a street, shooting at the roofs of the surrounding houses. He was getting a great kick out of watching the red tile disintegrate before his BAR. In my anger I went over him like a piece of sandpaper with a tongue lashing that he would not soon forget. He apologized and promised to stick close from then on.

At times we rode on top of the tanks, for this helped the poor, weary feet of the tired foot soldier. At one place my old friend, Charley Kruse, was killed instantly by six bullets in the back. They were six American bullets, fired from an American automatic weapon, accidently discharged by an American soldier. I could picture the telegram that his parents would receive in two weeks or so: "The Secretary of War desires me to express his deep regret that your son Pvt. Kruse Charles B. was killed in action in Germany 9 April 1945."

In the same skirmish, our hero Kelly was virtually blown apart by a hand grenade which went off in the pocket of his field jacket. Apparently the cotterpin had fallen out of the handle and had set off the fuse.

We received a report that the town ahead was well defended. With no other company in reserve, our company was split up; one half remained in a small grove of trees to give our half support should we need it. We started across an open field, but within a hundred yards of the town we were forced to take to a water-filled ditch for protection from the small-arms fire.

For a long time we lay in the cold water, waiting for aid which never came. Then the mortar shells began to splatter about in the soft mud.

"Frank!" yelled the lieutenant angrily. "Go back and see what the hell's wrong! Get us some help from somewhere!"

I breathed good-by to everything. It would be suicide, pure and simple. At least a dozen bullets whined each time one of us moved a muscle. I could never hope to make it.

With great effort, drawing much fire, I managed to get turned around in the ditch. Then I surveyed the situation.

My first move would be to make it to a railroad track some two hundred yards distant. With all the energy that I could muster I reared up and ran like a deer, in a low crouch. I could hear rifles and machine guns open up and the ground about me was being filled with bullets. As I approached the tracks, I could see sparks flying from the rails, the steel crossties, and the gravel in between. With one leap I hurled my body across the tracks and into a ditch on the other side. It was only by a miracle that I made it. The sermon by "Holy Joe," as we called our chaplain, must have had something behind it.

The enemy would have their weapons trained on the spot where I went down, so to fool them I crawled down the tracks a short distance before raising up to make another survey. Still they managed to put some shots in too close for comfort. Some of them passed right through the steel railroad tracks.

I crawled down a bit farther, dashed back across the tracks, covered a small open space, and then into the grove of trees. There the rest of the company rested, waiting to hear from us. They had not known that we needed help. In short order I made them understand that we did.

They circled about and came to bear upon the town from the other side. The enemy, seeing pressure coming from both front and side, retreated.

That same afternoon we came upon a well-entrenched force that turned twenty-millimeter antiaircraft guns on us. We were forced to take cover in a small wooded area on the crest of a hill. They were firing three kinds of shells—the steel armor-piercing slug, the tracer, and the silver-tipped type that exploded. The noise that those six weapons made was terrific, and the humming shrapnel sounded like a thousand swarms of bees as it flew about.

A popping noise above me made me understand that a fast-firing machine gun had been zeroed in on me. A few seconds after each burst passed over, I could hear the hum of the machine gun that fired them. It did not chatter and rattle but was as smooth as the engine of a fine automobile.

For me there was nothing to do but remain flat and wait for someone else to take care of it. I lay there with my cheek flat against the earth. I dared not raise up, for they passed over too close. The leaves rustled about me, the twigs fell from the low-hanging branches, and I could see the trees become white as they lost their bark from the twenty-millimeter guns.

I could see Boblo raise up after each burst. We all knew that it took the enemy twenty seconds to change barrels, which he had to do quite often. Boblo had located the weapon and was now waiting for his chance. I could see him get his BAR aimed, and then he ducked again to wait another turn.

The chance came. Boblo's automatic rifle barked out, and the machine gunner was put out of action for good.

While waiting for artillery to help us out we maneuvered for a better position. I came upon a red communication wire and quickly cut it. The twenty-millimeter guns opened up again. Boblo was caught standing. An explosive shell hit him in the stomach, and he dropped to his knees, trying to push his dangling intestines back into the gaping hole. He looked over at me with knowing eyes; this was our last stand together. I crawled over to him. The flying shells did not bother me, for to me the entire world had stopped; it was in mourning for a great hero and soldier. The American army had lost a brave warrior which it could never replace. Only the day before he had received a Certificate of Merit for a deed that would have netted a field grade officer at least the Silver Star. Now he lay here dying. For this his mother would be sent the Purple Heart.

The artillery came in, the enemy gave ground, and we captured their first sergeant. The lieutenant questioned him, but he would give no information.

"I am fighting for my country!" he screamed. "I love my country, and I love my leader!"

"Who is your leader?" asked the lieutenant.

"Adolf Hitler—yet," he answered.

The lieutenant turned to a colored soldier standing near-by. "Take him away, Smoky."

The pair hardly had disappeared into the bushes, when we heard the chatter of a grease gun. The colored soldier reappeared.

"What happened, Smoky?" asked the lieutenant.

"He tried to escape."

We all knew differently, but it was better to get rid of the fanatics than to have our sons over here in another twenty-five years.

I captured one of the gunners of a still hot twenty-millimeter gun. A camouflage cape hung from his shoulders to the ground, so I ordered him to remove it. As he did, it exposed American paratrooper boots and an Ordnance Department wrist watch.

I remembered the paratroopers who were hanging in the trees of France, the beaten and starved Americans who were prisoners of war, and the smoking twenty-millimeter guns that were unlawful to be used on ground personnel. To my comrades and me these were crimes which could not be forgiven. The working over that we had just received made us burn for revenge.

With my left foot I pushed him to the ground. As he lay there on his back, I questioned him. The muzzle of my rifle was a few inches from his face.

"Where did you get these?" I asked, pointing to the shoes and watch.

"Some of my comrades gave them to me."

"You lie!"

He grinned back rather arrogantly, then raised up on his elbows. My face burned with anger. I shot him through the forehead, and his head thumped back against the ground. With the butt of my rifle, I proceeded to crush it. I would make sure that this criminal paid for his misdeeds.

In the wee hours of the morning a patrol of four of us started out from the little village which we were holding. Hardly ten minutes away, on a macadam road, we heard the moan of a heavy shell coming in. Throughout the night we had been shelled by one hundred and fifty-five millimeter shells. This sounded a bit different, but I thought that it probably had a loose ring and would pass on over.

It landed just a few feet short of the road, to my right. It was a larger shell than the others. The blast blew me twenty feet from the road into an open field. I jumped up, partially deafened and dazed, and stumbled back onto the road. I had to complete my mission. I had to continue on my way. I saw the others sprawled upon the road behind, but they did not bother me. With a clear mind I would have turned back.

A few steps farther I heard the whistling scream again. I started to go down, but my senses had been numbed, so I did not react fast enough. It hit while I was still in a crouch. This time I landed in a water-filled ditch beside the road. I struggled to get up but seemed to be paralyzed. My limbs tingled and felt helpless as if they were asleep. My nose and throat burned terribly from sulphur fumes.

Two more shells came in. I could see their bright

236

flashes and hear the high flying shrapnel clank upon the road long after the explosions.

Then I thought of my fate. What a place to be caught, so helpless and so alone. I hugged my rifle closely and gripped it tightly as everything passed into oblivion.

X.

IT seemed like a deep sleep from which I had trouble awakening. At first I could see the all-white ceiling overhead. Had Saint Peter been good to me and let me in?

Later I realized that I was struggling, and was being held down by an American soldier and a poorly clad civilian girl. Had I been taken prisoner? Had this other soldier been taken prisoner and forced to work in this enemy hospital? The girl spoke French, which really had me puzzled.

"Take it easy, Joe," the soldier told me calmly. "You are in an American hospital. I am a ward boy, and she is a Belgian slave laborer who works here for her keep."

How different this was from the usual movie version of regaining consciousness with a beautiful nurse holding one's hand.

I took inventory of myself. My right arm and leg were in casts; I was hard of hearing in my right ear and had the worst case of halitosis that the world had ever known. The ward boy informed me that I had no broken bones, but my right leg and right arm had been operated on and several pieces of shrapnel were removed. My right eardrum was punctured and my lungs severely burned by the fumes I had inhaled.

238

He showed me the X-ray negatives. They looked as if they had been sprinkled with pepper. Thousands of dustlike particles of shrapnel were buried just beneath the skin. One surprising fact was that I had been wounded on Friday. This was Monday.

For the next long weeks, I went through the routine of sulfa pills, penicillin, and physical therapy. Every third day they passed a strong magnet over my body to remove the fine steel dust that was gradually coming to the surface of my measlelike skin. From my bed I saw the motion picture "Meet Me in St. Louis."

As time went by I passed back along the chain of hospitals and then up through the replacement pools. At this time they called them reenforcement pools. I saw the statue of Beethoven in the city of Bonn. The trees and iron benches in the park about him were scarred by the war. The war was over now. For me it had not come too soon. I was fed up with it, sick with it. Never again did I want to fight. I was the most peace-loving man in the world.

When I got back to the company, they were guarding highways, bridges, and even a large castle. In their spare moments they got drunk on Kümmel, from charred wooden barrels.

Loud noises frightened me. I jumped and jerked with each one. At night I had terrifying nightmares of combat. I grabbed my rifle, leaped out of bed, and squatted, on guard, in a corner of the room. The others sneaked up and jumped me. Then I returned to bed once again.

Before long the company commander had me transferred to the Military Police, for I was no longer fit for combat, either mentally or physically.

With the Military Police I moved to Berlin. There, in between times, I enjoyed the Palast Theatre and the Club Femina, while I argued with the Russians and fought the black market. Once I received a pass to Paris, where I proceeded to make the town. By taking the Metro to Trocadero I managed to see the American airplane display beneath the Eiffel Tower. Then I took the elevator up the tower where I enjoyed an evening of champagne, drinking, and dancing.

On the train which took us from Paris to Kassel, a displaced Slav, dressed in American army clothing, boarded our boxcar. During the night he was caught stealing a pistol from an infantryman who was sleeping. The infantryman awoke and gave fight. In the brief scuffle the Slav was pushed out of the boxcar as the train passed through a tunnel. I heard him yell as he thumped against the side of the tunnel and then back against the train.

On the way to Berlin the train was stopped by armed Russian soldiers. They used our engine as a switch engine for five hours. When it was nearly out of coal they returned it.

One grand autumn day, my day to be returned had come. I said good-by to the men of the Military Police Platoon with whom I had spent my time, climbed aboard a truck, and watched Steglitz and Berlin fade away.

For several days, while awaiting a ship, I stayed at the Kasserne in Grohn and stood guard duty on the Vegesack ferry. Then I was sent to Bremerhaven and homeward.

After two weeks of rough ocean voyage, the ship slipped into New York Harbor. It was evening and we had to wait at anchor until morning to unload. Once again I was home! I weighed thirty pounds less and was very nervous, but I was home! Home again! I should have been jubilant, but I could not be. I was just in a happy stupor.

The beautiful buildings stood majestically against the skyline with not a brick out of place. It was much better to have fought a war in someone else's back yard than in our own mighty United States. It was much better to have supplied arms and ammunition to foreign men who wished to fight on our side. Paying ten thousand dollars in supplies was much better than paying it in insurance for a dead American.

As I looked at the lights and watched the cars flying up and down the amber-lighted highway, tears came to my eyes. "Welcome home; thanks for a job well done." Yes, we had helped to do the job, but many were not here who had given more. To them we should all be forever grateful. As long as I lived, I would never forget my brothers-in-arms, who fell like leaves from the trees among which they fought. The memory of them would stay with me forever and a day—it had been etched in purple.

The Author

Born in Detroit in 1922, Frank J. Irgang was briefly a schoolteacher, a blast-furnace operator, and a college student before being drafted in December 1942. At first assigned to the Medical Corps, he soon became a regular combat infantryman and later served on special duty as a scout. He saw combat in Normandy, the Ardennes, the Rhineland, and Central Europe. His decorations include the Combat Infantryman Badge, the Purple Heart, and the Bronze Star.

After the war, Irgang worked as a shipping clerk, a salesman, and a store manager. In 1946, he married Virginia Daniger. He received a bachelor's degree from Central Michigan University, taught high school for three years, and then did his graduate studies in Industrial Technology at the University of Michigan, receiving a master's degree and a doctorate. In 1956, Dr. Irgang accepted a position at San Diego State University, where he taught for twenty-six years, eventually serving as chairman of the Department of Industrial Studies. Dr. Irgang is also the author of two novels, *The Wyandotte* and *Beneath the Snows of Stalingrad*. He and his wife reside in San Diego.

CPSIA information can be obtained
at www.ICGtesting.com
Printed in the USA
LVHW04s1949140718
583781LV00001B/46/P